INFORMATION SYSTEMS TECHNOLOGY

Desktop Dictionary of INFORMATION SYSTEMS TECHNOLOGY

Albert G. Giordano, Ph.D.

Professor Emeritus
Monterey Peninsula College
Monterey, California

Christine Disney

Author, Lecturer, Software and
Computer Consultant

Longman Business Education
520 North Dearborn Street
Chicago, Illinois 60610-4975

Published in the United States of America by
Longman Business Education, a division of
Longman Group USA Inc.

Adapted from *Information Technology Dictionary*
published by Pitman Publishing Limited, London, 1986.

Printed in the United States of America.

89 90 91 10 9 8 7 6 5 4 3 2 1

Acquisitions Editor: Barbara Wood Donner
Development Editor: Margaret Anne Schmidt
Cover Designer: Phil Kantz

Library of Congress Cataloging-in-Publication Data

Giordano, Al, 1925-
Desktop dictionary of information systems technology / Albert G. Giordano, Christine Disney.
p. cm.
Adapted from: Information technology dictionary. 1986.
ISBN 0-88462-840-X : $14.95
1. Electronic data processing—Dictionaries. 2. Information technology—Dictionaries. I. Disney, Christine. II. Giordano, Al, 1925- Information technology dictionary. III. Title.
QA76.15.G585 1989
004'.03'21—dc19 88-27236
CIP

Preface

During the past 35 years, the development of office systems technology to process information has moved from sequal manual operations printing and publishing to a range of more sophisticated services and facilities based on inexpensive microelectronic components.

By the late 1970's, the term Information Systems Technology (usually abbreviated to IST) was being used to refer to both the coordinated and individual aspects of modern electronic technology used for information handling.

IST incorporates computing, telecommunications, word processing, consumer electronics, and broadcasting. Its applications are business, educational, industrial, international commerce, office administration, medical and scientific, legal and professional, and personal home use.

Albert G. Giordano
January 1, 1989.

Introduction

This dictionary contains more than 2,400 terms related to data processing, computing, secretarial sciences, office management, and other aspects of information handling.

All of these terms relate to information systems technology: the acquisition, production, transformation, storage, and transmission of data by electronic means in vocal, pictorial, textual, or numeric form.

This book is arranged in alphabetical sections, each word or phrase included in letter-by-letter order. Abbreviations and acronyms appear in the order of their characters, rather than in the order of the words they stand for.

Abbreviations and acronyms also appear in the special appendix at the back of the book.

Many words are cross-referenced. Technical terms are highlighted with italics. Italicized terms appear as entries in the dictionary.

A number of fundamental terms that occur frequently are listed below. Users of this dictionary should familiarize themselves with the meanings of these terms:

application
bit
character
communication
computer
data
data processing
database
device
disk
field
file
hardware
information processing
language
magnetic disk
magnetic tape
memory
network
nucleus
peripheral
printer
processor
program
programming
record
semiconductor
software
store
storage
system
telecommunications
terminal
word processing
workstation

A

A Programming Language (APL) A scientific *programming language,* using a specially designed *character set,* with applications in advanced mathematical work.

abnormal termination A termination to a process brought about by the *operating system* when the process reaches a point from which it cannot continue.

abort To undergo or cause *abnormal termination.*

AC See *alternating current.*

a.c. voltage The force that causes *alternating current* to flow through an electrical *conductor.*

acceptance testing This *testing* is normally under the control of the procurers of a system, and is designed to ensure that the system is suitable for operational use.

access mechanism The physical unit composed of the *read/write heads* of a *direct access storage device.*

access time This is the time taken to retrieve information from a *storage location.* The information may be computer *program instructions* or data for a particular application.

accumulator A register inside the *CPU* that holds results of arithmetic operations.

ACIA See *asynchronous communications interface adapter.*

acoustic Relating to sound.

acoustic coupler A type of *modem* that converts serial digital data into a sound signal that can be transmitted down telephone lines. Ideal for connecting portable terminals to *remote* computers, two tones are used to define the bits 0 and 1.

acoustic hood A box that covers a printer to deaden the noise it makes.

acronym Many aspects of *Information Systems Technology* are described by acronyms that are words or groups of letters taken from the first letters of the item they describe, *e.g.* **BASIC** for **B**eginners' **A**ll-purpose **S**ymbolic **I**nstruction **C**ode.

activity chart A chart used to describe the breakdown of the structure of a department by specifying what each person does. It provides the *systems analyst* with an indication of the hours involved in the completion of work.

actuator The actuator of a *disk drive* is the mechanism that causes the *read/write heads* to be moved to the desired *track*.

A/D Analog to digital. See *analog-digital converter.*

ADC See *analog-digital converter.*

ADCCP See *Advanced Data Communication Control Procedure.*

adder A circuit that takes two digits as inputs and outputs their sum.

adding machine The first true adding machine was invented in 1642 by Blaise Pascal. The numbers to be added were entered on dials and the result read from dial positions. Electronic calculators replaced electric adding machines.

address The identification of a *store location.*

address bus The portion of the *system bus* that carries the address of *memory* or *I/O port* to be accessed.

address machine Traditionally using metal stencils or embossed metal plates for a name and address, the addressing machine prints onto envelopes or adhesive labels. Modern systems are based on *microprocessor* technology in which names and addresses are held on flexible *magnetic media* that can be amended easily. Speeds of printing can approach 9000 addresses per hour.

address modification Changing of the address portion of a machine language instruction by means of an operation on the instruction.

address space A function of the addressing range. If a computer has a 16-bit address range, the address space may be up to 64 k-bytes in length.

address word A microprocessor word that contains only the address of a memory location.

administrative secretary A secretary who is responsible for managerial tasks.

administrative supervisor A person who manages administrative secretaries.

ADP Automatic data processing. See *data processing*.

Advanced Data Communication Control Procedure (ADCCP) A bit-orientated *data link* control *protocol* developed by *ANSI* and similar to *SDLC* and *HDLC*.

Advanced Manufacturing Technology (AMT) See *computer aided/assisted design, computer aided/assisted manufacturing* and *computer integrated manufacturing*.

Advanced Research Projects Agency Network (ARPANET) The collection of *host computers* plus network making up the first major *packet switching* network.

advanced text management This component of *electronic office* facilities includes proofreading, *hyphenation* and *language translation.*

aerial A device used for receiving or transmitting *electromagnetic radiation* at radio frequencies.

AFIPS See *American Federation of Information Processing Societies, Inc.*

AHPL A Hardware Programming Language.

AI See *artificial intelligence.*

ALGOL See *algorithmic language.*

algorithm A prescribed set of well defined rules giving a sequence of operations for the solution of a problem.

algorithmic language (ALGOL) A *high level programming language* developed in Europe around 1958. ALGOL60 is a problem solving language designed for mathematical and scientific use. ALGOL68, designed in 1968, is a more powerful language for a variety of uses.

alignment choice Most *word processors* provide the choice of two different text alignments: *justified text* or *ragged text.*

alphanumeric An alphanumeric character is any of the 26 letters in the Roman alphabet or any of the decimal digits, zero to nine.

alter A modification of the contents of an accumulator or extend bit.

alternating current (AC) A flow of electricity that reaches maximum in one direction, decreases to zero then reverses itself and reaches a maximum in the opposite direction. The cycle is repeated continuously. The number of cycles per second is equal to the *frequency,* *e.g.* 50Hz or 60Hz.

alternator A device that produces an alternating *voltage.*

ALU See *arithmetic and logic units.*

AMA See *automatic message accounting.*

ambient temperature range The range of environmental temperatures, in the vicinity of a device, over which the device may be operated safely and within specifications. For forced air cooled devices, the ambient temperature is measured at the air intake.

American Federation of Information Processing Societies, Inc. (AFIPS) An organization founded in 1961 to provide a structure for societies and associations interested in information processing to join together to advance the state of the art.

American National Standards Institute (ANSI) An organization founded in 1918 to support industry standards. It establishes US industrial standards and their correspondence to those set by *ISO*. ANSI determines hardware-related standards and some software standards.

American Society of Mechanical Engineers (ASME) The society responsible for the development of the ASME work study *flowchart* symbols used in systems investigation and analysis.

American Standard Code for Information Interchange (ASCII, pronounced ASK-ee) A standard character encoding scheme introduced in 1963 and used widely on many machines. An ASCII document is unformatted (no indents, boldfaces, tab stops, etc.) and can usually be read by any word processing program.

amplifier A device that receives an input signal and gives as output a magnified version of the signal.

amplitude The strength of a *current* or *signal.*

amplitude modulation The *amplitude* of the carrier signal is varied. This form of *modulation* is not often directly used in computer communication.

AMT Advanced manufacturing technology. See *computer aided/assisted design, computer aided/assisted manufacturing* and *computer integrated manufacturing.*

analog Having to do with continuous electronic signals used for information transmission.

analog computer A computer that performs computations by manipulating continuous physical variables such as *voltage.*

analog-digital converter (ADC) A device that can accept an *analog signal* and produce an equivalent *digital signal.* Compare *DAC.*

analog signal A smoothly varying value of *voltage* or *current, i.e.* a signal that varies continuously in *amplitude* and time. It often represents a physical quantity. Compare *digital signal.*

ancestral file system A way of classifying and storing electronic files. The three most recent versions of a file are labeled grandfather, father, and son. These are retained for security purposes.

AND function This function combines statements such that the outcome is only true (1) if all statements are true (1); otherwise the outcome is false (0).

AND gate An electronic logic device that performs according to the *AND function, i.e.* all inputs must be (1) to produce an output of (1).

annotation Explanation added to a program to assist the reader. It is frequently in the form of comments within the program text.

ANSI See *American National Standards Institute.*

answering/recording machine A machine that 'answers' the telephone when a subscriber is out or busy. Modern versions are often included in a workstation where a *microprocessor* enables a single piece of equipment to provide automatic answering, call recording, telephone directory lists, *autodial* and loudspeaker facilities with local computer processing.

antennae See *aerial.*

APL See *A Programming Language.*

append To add new information at the end of an existing document or file.

application The task or group of tasks for which the computer is being used.

application packages A set of specialized programs and associated *documentation* to carry out a particular application, *e.g.* payroll.

application program Any user-written software that is run on a microcomputer.

application software *Programs* or *modules* directed at some class of application, such as word processing or accounting.

applications terminal A combination of input and output devices configured into a unit to meet the requirements of a particular type of business activity and environment, *e.g. point of sale terminals.*

APT See *automatically programmed tools.*

architecture See *machine architecture.*

archive To hold in long-term storage.

archived file A copy of a file held for safety outside the computing system.

argument A variable factor, the value of which sets the value of the function of which it is a part.

arithmetic and logic unit (ALU) The part of the *CPU* where arithmetic and logic operations are performed. Sometimes called the arithmetic unit.

arithmetic error A type of *run time error* that can be detected by the *operating system, e.g.* attempting to put information into the *array* location 11 when there is only a 10 *element* list.

arithmetic operator A type of *operator* that denotes one of the operations of arithmetic, *e.g.* +, −, * (multiplication), and / (divide).

ARPANET See *Advanced Research Projects Agency Network.*

array A set of *storage locations* referred to by a single identifier. Individual *elements* are referenced by combining one or more *subscripts* with the identifier name, e.g. STOCK(3,5). Also any element may be referenced with respect to the start *address* of the first element.

artificial intelligence (AI) A discipline concerned with the building of computer programs that perform tasks that require intelligence when done by humans.

ASCC Automatic Sequence Controlled Calculator, 1944. See *Harvard Mark 1.*

ASCII See *American Standard Code for Information Interchange.*

ASCII control characters A group of nonprintable ASCII characters used to control a peripheral device or send messages from one machine to another.

ASME See *American Society of Mechanical Engineers.*

aspect ratio The ratio of the width of a *television* picture to the height. 4:3 has been adopted by the UK and many other countries.

ASR Automatic send and receive.

assembler A program that takes as input a program written in *assembly language* and translates it into *machine code* or *relocatable code.*

assembly code A set of codes used by a programmer when writing programs in an *assembly language.*

assembly language A *low level programming language* that is easier to use than *machine code.* It generally uses symbolic addresses that are translated into machine code by an *assembler.* One assembly language *instruction* becomes one machine code instruction.

assign To reserve a part of the computer system, *e.g.* a printer, for use by the program during its running.

assignment An operation that places a value in the *store location* corresponding to a given *variable.*

Association for Computer Machinery (ACM) A U.S. organization founded in 1947 for these purposes: to advance the sciences and arts of information processing; to promote the free interchange of information among specialists and the public; and to maintain the integrity and competence of individuals engaged in information processing.

astable multivibrator See *multivibrator.*

asynchronous Pertaining to actions and events that are not correlated with some reference time.

asynchronous communications interface adapter (ACIA) An *integrated circuit* that can be used in *data communication* interfaces.

asynchronous data transmission (start-stop mode) The sending of data such that synchronized timing between sending and receiving devices is not necessary for successful communication. Timing is accomplished by signals indicating the beginning and end of each byte.

asynchronous mode An operational mode that requires a form of control timing in which a specific operation is initiated by the receipt of an indication (signal) that the preceding operation has been completed. See also *synchronous mode.*

ATL automated tape library.

Atlas The first computer to incorporate the many features now considered standard. The prototype was operating in 1961 and production models appeared in 1963.

ATM See *automatic teller machines.*

attenuation The reduction in *amplitude* of a signal when it passes through a medium that dissipates its energy. It is usually measured in decibels.

attribute The property of an *entity* within files and data bases. When a record provides information about an entity, a field will correspond to an attribute.

audio conference A meeting held in various locations, using voice communication (telephone) to connect the participants. It is also possible that *facsimile transmission* facilities will be provided.

audit trail A means of identifying actions performed upon data by tracing data on a source document to an output such as a report.

authentication of messages The use of *electronic signature* techniques to ensure the message recipient can accurately verify the identity of the message sender.

author The person who has initiated a document, *i.e.* the originator.

author language A generic term for *programming languages* that allow users to create learning materials without any detailed programming knowledge.

authority list A list of terms (used as *keywords)* that can be used by people compiling text oriented databases and by those wishing to search those databases.

authorization Providing permission to access computer systems.

auto start The facility to load automatically a specific program or *utility* when a computer is switched on, *e.g.* loading the BASIC *interpreter* into memory when a *microcomputer* is switched on.

autocode An early programming language designed to remove some of the constraints of having to program in *machine code* or *assembler.*

autodial A device on a videotex terminal that automatically dials a prerecorded telephone number for connection to a videotex computer.

automated office See *electronic office.*

automated tape library (ATL) A peripheral device in which a large number of cartridges or reels of magnetic tape are held in a storage area that can be accessed automatically.

automatic calling unit (ACU) A device that allows a computer or terminal to originate telephone calls over the public switched network. Computer networks that use ACUs usually function as *store and forward systems* for message switching.

automatic carriage return After setting left and right hand margins, a word processing operator has no need to use the carriage return key.

automatic code A technique used by programmers wherein the microcomputer itself is used to code programs.

automatic data capture Automatically collecting data for a particular computer process, *e.g.* temperature in a chemical process, meter readings in a *wired society.*

automatic data processing (ADP) See *data processing.*

automatic message accounting (AMA) Refers to the procedures for collecting information about telephone calls to provide subscriber bills. The computer records 'time on' and 'time off' details for calculating a charge.

automatic repeat The ability of a key to repeat its function if continuously depressed.

Automatic Sequence Controlled Calculator (1944) (ASCC) See *Harvard Mark 1.*

automatic telephone exchange A telephone exchange where electromechanical relays and switches have been replaced by computer controlled exchanges (see *digital exchange).*

automatic teller machines (ATM) Equipment, usually placed in shops and other public places, to facilitate an automatic debit from the buyer's account and corresponding credit to the seller's account by the banking network.

automatically programmed tools (APT) A language developed for the *numerical control* of machine tools.

automaton A device that mechanically processes an input instruction with the aim of deciding whether the instruction is valid or not, thereby producing an appropriate output response. Inputs and outputs can be instructions, signals or movements.

auto-repeat facility A feature of certain electronic keyboards in which a character is automatically repeated if the key is held down for a period of time.

autotest program An operating system program designed to help the programmer test and debug programs.

auto-verify Providing automatic *verification* facilities on punch-verify equipment.

auxiliary operation An operation performed by equipment not under direct control of the central processing unit.

auxiliary storage device A storage facility in addition to the computer's RAM. See also *backing store.*

B

back end processor A processor that is used for some specialized function such as a *database management system* or a special purpose *arithmetic and logic unit.*

background activity Low priority programs running on a multiprogramming system.

background processing The process within a *time sharing* system that enables less urgent tasks to utilize time which is not required by critical tasks. For example, in a word processing system, documents may be printed when the processor is not dealing directly with user text manipulation. See also *foreground processing.*

backing store The *memory/storage* device on which information is held for reference but not for direct execution.

backspace code A machine function that allows the operator to backspace the recording medium without affecting the text.

backspace key A key which, when pressed, makes the *cursor* move one position to the left. It is sometimes marked delete.

back-up A replica made of something such as a data disk for reasons of safety. It will normally be stored separately from the original source material so that both are not lost or damaged.

back-up copy See *back-up.*

back-up store See *backing store.*

badge reader A device designed to read information encoded into a small plastic card.

bank switching A technique allowing computers with small address spaces to extend their address range in multiples of the address-space size.

bar chart Sometimes called a Gantt chart, a bar chart usually consists of horizontal bars that indicate the progress of activities listed down the left hand column with the passage of time.

bar code A printed machine readable code that consists of parallel bars of varied width and spacing. The codes on household goods consist of 30 bars providing a unique 13-digit code number for each product.

bar code reader A device that will read *bar codes.*

barrel printer A type of solid font *line printer* in which the *font* is etched or engraved on the outer surface of a cylinder that extends across the full width of the line to be printed. See also *drum printer.*

base Another name for the radix of a positional number system. Hence decimal numbers are base 10 numbers and binary numbers are base 2 numbers.

base two See *binary.*

baseplate An interface device that enables an electric typewriter to be converted to a low level word processor.

BASIC (Beginner's all-purpose symbolic instruction code) An easy programming language popular with many beginning computer students.

batch control The control sequences carried out manually or by computer to check data submitted to *batch processing* systems.

batch processing A technique in which computer processing does not begin until all the input (data and/or programs) has been collected together, *i.e.* batched.

batch programming A method of executing programs whereby each is read into the system in order (for sequential execution).

baud rate The number of times per second that a system, especially a data *transmission channel,* changes state. In the particular case of a *binary* channel, the baud rate is equal to the bit rate, i.e. 1 baud = 1 bit per second. The rate was named after J. M. E. Baudot.

Baudot code A five character code used for Telex messages.

BCD See *binary coded decimal.*

BCPL A systems *programming language* that incorporates the control structures needed for *structured programming.*

BDOS Basic disk operating system. An abbreviation for the CP/M nucleus. See also *nucleus.*

beginning of tape (BOT) A physical marker of a magnetic tape by which the *tape transport* senses the start of the part of the tape which has been recorded or which may be used for data recording. The beginning of the tape must be long enough to allow a tape to be loaded and threaded on the transport. See also *EOT.*

belt printer See *band printer.*

benchmark A problem or task that has been designed to evaluate the performance of a system (hardware and software). In a benchmark test, a system is subjected to a known workload and the performance of the system against this workload is measured.

bi-chrome ribbon A typewriter ribbon having two colors, usually black and red.

bidirectional printer A printer that increases speed by printing when moving in both directions across a page.

binary The binary or base two number system consists of two digits, 0 and 1. This is the number system most commonly used in computers as it conveniently represents the presence or absence of *digital signals.*

binary arithmetic Arithmetic performed on numbers represented in *binary notation.*

binary chop search A binary search *algorithm* that starts with a file having *sortkeys* in ascending order. The middle record is examined and depending upon whether this is less or greater than the desired key, the top or bottom part of the file is again examined. Continuing in this way, the algorithm either finds the desired record or discovers its absence from the file.

binary coded decimal (BCD) A code in which a string of *binary digits* represents a decimal digit. In the natural binary coded decimal (NBCD) system, each decimal digit 0 to 9 is represented by the string of 4 bits whose value is equivalent to the decimal digit, *e.g.* 3 is represented by 0011 and 9 by 1001. The NBCD code is the 8421-code such that the weighted sum of the bits in a codeword is equal to the coded decimal digit.

binary counter A circuit using a group of flip-flops to convert a series of pulses into binary form.

binary digit See *bit.*

binary notation A system of number representation using the two digits 0 and 1.

binary number See *binary.*

binary program A program in which all information is in binary microcomputer language.

binary scale Each position in a binary number corresponds to a power of 2, *i.e.* 1, 2, 4, 8, 16, 32, 64, 128, 256.

binary search See *binary chop search.*

BIO Byte-oriented input/output. See also *input/output.*

BIOS Basic input/output system. See also *input/output.*

biotechnology The technology of processing living cells, *e.g.* to provide economic methods of producing organic chemicals or sources of energy.

bipolar transistor A semiconductor device having three electrodes. It is effectively a sandwich of two types of *doped semiconductor,* usually *p-type* and *n-type* silicon and so contains two p-n junctions. When the region common to both junctions is p-type, an npn *transistor* is formed; when it is n-type, an pnp transistor is formed. Bipolar transistor *switches,* working into saturation, are the basis of *TTL* circuits.

biquinary code A seven-bit binary code with the weights 5, 0, 4, 3, 2, 1 and 0 respectively. Each combination of the code contains only two 1-bits. For example, the decimal numeral 3 is 0101000.

biquinary system The Roman number system of providing a different symbol for each power of 10 and for five times each power of 10, *e.g.* 1 = 1, 10 = X, 100 = C and 5 × 1 = V, 5 × 10 = L, 5 × 100 = D.

bistable multivibrator See *multivibrator.*

bisynchronous communications A high-speed convention, or mode, for transmitting information electronically.

bit (binary digit) A number having the value of either 0 or 1 in binary arithmetic (compared with the value of 0 through 9 in decimal arithmetic). A bit is the smallest unit of information used by the computer.

bit density A physical specification referring to the number of bits that can be recorded per unit of length or area.

bit rate The number of bits transmitted or transferred per unit of time. The unit of time is usually one second, hence bits per second (bps). See also *baud rate.*

bits per second (bps) See *bit rate.*

bit-serial One bit at a time, as opposed to bit-parallel, in which all bits of a character can be handled simultaneously.

black box A concept used to depict the main roles of components within a system without the confusing detail of each individual component.

blackout The total loss of commercial power.

block A collection of data units, such as *words,* characters or records that are stored in adjacent physical positions in memory or on a peripheral storage device. A block can therefore be treated as a single unit whereby data can be transferred between storage device and memory, using a single *instruction.* Blocks may be fixed or variable in size. In word processing applications blocks of text may be manipulated within a document.

block diagram A diagram that represents graphically the interconnection relationships between elements of a computer system. It usually consists of squares or rectangles labeled to represent different hardware and software components with lines showing any interconnections.

block operation Any operation that is performed upon a *block* unit.

board A flat silicon sheet about 5 × 10 inches, with printed circuitry that adds to the computer's ability. IBM personal computers and some Apple Macintoshes have slots where users can add boards to upgrade the system's capabilities.

boilerplate A sentence, paragraph, or other amount of text that is used repeatedly without change (such as the standard closing of a business letter).

Boolean algebra A set of rules for manipulating truth values according to truth tables. Truth tables reflect the state of an electrical signal after different *logic gates* have been combined to form an electrical circuit.

Boolean operator (logic gate) One of the *AND, OR, NAND, NOR* or *NOT* functions.

Boolean value Either of the two logical values TRUE or FALSE that indicates a truth value. They usually take the values 1 and 0 respectively in a binary system.

boot To start up a computer or a program.

booting An automatic process for ensuring the computer is in a state ready for use. Booting may be linked to the switch that turns the equipment on, or a required special combination of key sequences.

boot-load To load the operating system into the computer after cold-start power-up.

bootstrap The short program, usually stored in *ROM,* that will be processed when *booting* taking place.

BOT See *beginning of tape.*

BOT marker The beginning of tape marker is a physical feature on a magnetic tape by which the tape transport senses where to start reading or recording data. See also *EOT* marker.

bottom space The number of lines defined for being left blank at the bottom of a page of word processed text.

bounded media A category of transmission media that includes: twisted pairs of wires, *coaxial cables, waveguides, optical fibers.* See also *free space media.*

BPS Bits per second. See *bit rate.*

branch instructions Instructions that direct the microcomputer to leave the basic program and branch to another point in the same program.

breadboard An experimental circuit board that is used to try out possible circuits. Access to individual components is simple and hence the overall arrangement of prototype circuits can be easily modified.

breakpoint A temporary halt inserted in a program, in order for the *programmer* to inspect the contents of *registers, storage locations,* etc. to aid the *debug* process.

bridgeware Any software or hardware that eases the transition from the use of one computer system to another that is not entirely compatible.

broadband system A communication system that provides up to a 300 megahertz *bandwidth*. This enables many applications to share the same cable and, if required, transmit at different data rates.

broadcast data network An open ended network for sending and receiving data transmissions. Compare *ring data network, bus network* and *star network.*

broadcasting A message routing algorithm in which a message is transmitted to all *nodes* in a network. See also *multicasting.*

brownout A planned voltage reduction by an electricity supply station to counter excessive demand on their generation or distribution system.

bubble memory A type of digital memory in which data is represented by magnetic bubbles that are made to move through a stationary planar medium. Having no moving parts, the memory is more rugged than disk memory and is a *non-volatile memory.*

bubble sort A form of sorting by exchanging pairs of elements that are out of sequence. The exchange process is repeated throughout a file until no more pairs need exchanging.

bucket sort An external sort in which records to be sorted are grouped in some way and each group stored in a distinct 'bucket' ready for easy retrieval.

buffer A temporary holding location for data.

buffer register A register used for intermediate storage in the transfer sequence between the microcomputer and a peripheral device. (I/P device.)

buffered memory See *buffer.*

buffering The action of using a store area (*buffer*) to hold data temporarily.

bug An error or mistake in a program or system. It can also be a fault in equipment.

buggy A motorized device on wheels that is connected to a computer. It can be made to move under the control of a program that accepts *feedback* from the sensing mechanisms on the buggy, such as *photoelectric cells.*

bundled A term used by equipment suppliers whereby a single price is provided for a system that includes all necessary hardware and software components.

bureau An independent source of computing facilities (hardware and software) whose services may be hired to perform required jobs.

burst mode Transfer of all information in one data record from an input device to main storage in one operation.

burster A mechanism for separating continuous *fan-folded paper* into single sheets.

bus A physical signal carrier that connects several parts of a computer system. An abbreviation for *busbar.*

bus network A network that enables all nodes to be connected to a single communicating line. Information can travel in both directions and the control system determines which node can use the bus at any one time. Compare *ring data network* and *star network.*

busbar A heavy rigid electrical conductor used for high power feeders, *i.e.* it is common to several electrical loads and/or sources.

business game A simulation of a hypothetical business environment. The players act as competitors, deploying resources in the hope of gaining a large share of the market and developing management skills.

business system A set of related components that may consist of hardware, software, *documentation* and manual procedures for supporting business activities.

byte A set of binary digits (bits), usually representing one character, which are treated by the computer as one unit. A byte is a subdivision of a *word.*

byte-oriented input/output This portion of an operating system handles all byte- or character-oriented input/output operations for the nucleus.

C

C A programming language similar to PASCAL but more flexible; it allows the user to access hardware features.

cable A group of many wires bound together.

cable management Running wires and cables so as to prevent them from being unsightly or hazardous.

cable television Television receivers connected by cable to local distribution centers, *i.e.* reception is improved from a direct line connection compared to a variable reception from aerials receiving broadcast television. Originally provided to overcome broadcast reception problems, cable networks are being installed for an expected increase in the numbers of different commercial companies wishing to sell services that will be transmitted on specific cable channels. It also simplifies the development of a charging system that will be able to monitor and detect the use of each cable channel accurately. This is not feasible with broadcast television reception. In some systems it is possible to make a two-way channel connection that allows data to be sent from the receiver to the system controller via a *keypad* or direct linkup to a household device, *e.g.* electricity, gas and water meters.

cache memory An extremely fast part of *main store* that is used in high performance systems. It is inserted between the processor and memory proper.

CAD See *computer aided/assisted design.*

CAE See *computer aided/assisted engineering.*

CAFS See *contents addressable file store.*

CAI See *computer aided/assisted instruction.*

CAL See *computer aided/assisted learning.*

calculator An electronic device by means of which arithmetic operations can be performed on numbers entered from a keyboard. Final solutions and intermediate numbers are generally printed or displayed. *(LCD* or *LED* displays).

CALL See *computer aided/assisted language learning.*

call An explicit program statement requesting the use of a procedure.

CAM See *computer aided/assisted manufacturing.*

CAMA Centralized automatic message accounting. See *automatic message accounting.*

capacitance The property of a device by virtue of which a quantity of electricity has to be imparted to it to raise its potential above that of its surroundings.

capacitor An electrical device consisting of two conducting plates (electrodes) separated by a layer of insulating material. It will thus have an appreciable capacitance and each electrode carries a charge of electricity. If an *a.c. voltage* is applied to it, it will take a *current.*

carbon ribbon A printer ribbon made of thin plastic, coated with carbon. It gives a very high quality appearance, but is expensive and does not last very long. Compare *fiber ribbon.*

carbonless paper Paper that has been chemically treated to produce copies without the use of carbons.

card punch A device that punches holes in designated locations on cards that store data.

card reader A device consisting of a mechanical punched card reader and related electronic circuitry which transcribes data from punched cards to main storage.

card verify See *verification.*

cardphone A public telephone that accepts a slim *phonecard* instead of cash. Once a dialed number is connected, units are removed from the magnetically encoded phonecard until the units run out or the call is terminated. Phonecards are obtainable from any post office displaying the phonecard sign. (The cardphone system is used in many European countries.)

career path A progression of jobs leading to a lifetime work goal.

carriage return (CR) A key used to move the printer head or screen cursor to the extreme left hand side of the page/screen. It may also be used to mark the end of a line of text or number entry. Often called 'Return.'

carriage return/line feed (CR/LF) This key performs the same action as the *CR* together with a *line feed.* In some cases a terminal will be marked with a CR and CR/LF. The CR will be used to terminate data entry, *i.e.* send the data to the processor; and the CR/LF will be needed to end a line and produce a line feed on a display.

carrier See *modulation.*

carrier sense multiple access with collision detection (CSMA/CD) A data link control *protocol* applicable to a *broadcast data network* in which all stations can receive messages. A station can detect the presence of a transmitted message by sensing the *carrier* of the transmission. When a station wishes to send a message,

cartridge A container used to protect and facilitate the use of various computer media such as magnetic tape, magnetic disk or printer ribbon. It is usually designed so that the medium remains permanently within the cartridge and the medium itself is not touched by the operator. It may also be a removable module of software, often permanently stored as an *integrated circuit.*

cartridge disk See *cartridge.*

cartridge drive Either a *tape transport* for handling a tape *cartridge* or a *disk drive* for handling a disk cartridge.

cartridge ribbon A printer ribbon that is supplied in a *cartridge.*

cashless society A society of the future that does not require any metal or paper money. The technology required for cashless transactions is already available, *e.g. credit cards, smart cards, cardphones* and *electronic funds transfer systems.*

cassette A container similar to a *cartridge* but conventionally the term cassette is used for magnetic tapes that are interchangeable with a domestic audio cassette.

cassette tape See *cassette.*

cassette-based micro system A *microcomputer* system supplied with *cassette* tape *backing store.*

CAT See (1) *computer aided/assisted testing.* (2) *computer aided/assisted training.* See *computer based training.*

catalog See *directory.*

cathode ray tube (CRT) The normal television picture tube that is also used in *monitors* and *VDUs.* The main advantage of the CRT over the new flat screens is its superior brightness.

CBL See *computer based learning.*

CBMS See *computer based message system.*

CBT See *computer based training.*

cell A member of a *linked list.*

cellular radio An extension of the telephone communications provided for mobile (car based or hand held) terminals via *radio frequency* channels. The term cellular is used to signify that the area covered by the earlier network is divided into a large number of adjacent subareas or cells.

cellular telephone Wireless mobile telephone based on cellular technology, often used in automobiles and other vehicles.

centering A feature of most word processing software that places a line of text in the center of the available space between the margins.

central memory (CM) See *main store.*

central processing unit (CPU) The principal operating part of a computer. It is usually defined as the *arithmetic and logic unit* and the *control unit* and sometimes includes primary memory.

central processor See *central processing unit.*

centralized automatic message accounting (CAMA) See *automatic message accounting.*

centralized data processing The provision of computer processing facilities at some central location, to which other parts or subsidiaries of an organization send material for processing either via manual communication or telecommunication links. Compare *distributed processing.*

centralized system A system in which work is carried out in one central place.

centronics compatible A standard used to designate the connection of computers to printers for parallel signal transmission.

CGA/EGA Color graphics adapter/enhanced graphics adapter. The two principal standards for color monitors used with IBM computers.

chad The piece of material that is removed when holes are made in punch cards, paper tape or printer paper.

chain printer A type of *solid font line printer* in which the font is etched or engraved on small plates that are linked together to form a chain. It was superseded by the *train printer.*

chaining The action of automatically linking from one program which is being processed to a second program or segment that is held on file and needs to be transferred into memory. This technique is often used for programs that are too large to fit into the memory at one time.

changeover See *pilot operation, parallel running* and *direct changeover.*

changes file See *transaction file.*

channel Any physical path followed by data, particularly between a central processing unit and a peripheral device, *e.g.* between the user's program and a file on backing store.

character One of a set of symbols that may be represented in a computer. These can be letters, digits, spaces, punctuation marks, etc.

character delete A word processing system function which allows characters to be deleted as part of the editing process.

character printer A printer that prints each character in turn, *e.g. daisy wheel printer.* See also *line printer* and *serial printer.*

character recognition See *optical character recognition* and *magnetic ink character reading device.*

character set The set of characters that is handled by a specific machine.

character string A sequence of data bytes that represents characters in a code.

character-addressable Pertaining to a computer that performs operations on variable-length words.

characteristic See *normalization of data.*

characters per inch (CPI) (1) A measure of storage density of a magnetic tape. (2) Printing *pitch.*

characters per second (CPS) A measure of transmission or printing speed.

charged couple device (CCD) A recent technological innovation similar in concept to bubble memory; *i.e.* it utilizes charges in a memory crystal.

chart recorder A record keeping device that plots graphs by the movement of a pen to the right or left as a piece of paper is moved steadily in one direction under the bar track holding the pen. Frequently linked to sensors used for continuously monitoring environmental conditions such as temperature and humidity.

check bit A binary check digit associated with a computer word or a fixed-length group of characters for the purpose of detecting certain types of errors.

check digit An extra digit or other character that is attached to a number or code as a means of later checking the validity of the item. The choice of the extra character is based on an algorithm linking the rest of the characters. Check digits are primarily used to help avoid *transposition errors* and *transcription errors.*

check sum See *check total.*

check total A sum resulting from the addition of a specified field from each group of records, used for checking purposes. The process may also be applied to program code and blocks of data such that the possible corruption of stored items is checked every time the stored file is read and check totals are recalculated and stored whenever a file is written.

checkerboard An alternating pattern of *0*s and *1*s stored in a microcomputer for testing purposes.

checkpoint A place in a program where data is checked or recorded for restart purposes.

chip A small section of a single crystal of *semiconductor,* usually silicon, which is the basis of an *integrated circuit.*

chip card See *smart card.*

CIM See (1) *computer input microfilm;* (2) *computer integrated manufacturing.*

circuit The combination of a number of electrical devices and *conductors* that, when interconnected to form a conducting path, fulfill some desired function. Also a physical (electrical) connection used for communication. See also *integrated circuit.*

circuit board See *printed circuit.*

circuit switched network A network of communication lines that are linked to a switching center (exchange). The job of the switching center is to establish a short term link between any two lines connected to it. The existence of a temporary link between two or more parties is referred to as a call and the path between the calling and called parties is known as a *circuit.*

circular queue A series of stored documents that has a fixed number of entries that are reused circularly.

CIS-COBOL See *compact interactive standard-cobol.*

clear To reset all cells or elements of a device to zero.

clock The source of synchronizing impulses, usually a crystal-controlled oscillator.

cluster A group of workstations, often related in task or sharing common equipment.

CM Central memory. See *main store.*

CMI See *computer managed instruction.*

CML See *computer managed learning.*

coaxial cable A cable suitable for high *frequencies* where one of the *conductors* is surrounded by the second conductor with an insulating medium between.

COBOL See *Common Business Oriented Language.*

CODASYL See *Conference on Data Systems Languages.*

code A rule for transforming a message from one symbolic form into another. See also *encoder* and *decoder.* Also used to refer to a set of program instructions.

codec An abbreviation for coder/decoder, a device that converts a continuous analog signal into an encoded representation in a digital bit stream and vice versa. It is used in telephone systems to convert analog voice signals into digital signals. A codec is the inverse of a *modem.*

coding The action of producing *code, i.e.* writing program instructions.

coding form See *coding sheet.*

coding sheet A special form on which program instructions may be written. This form is especially useful for *languages* that require a special statement layout and for programs which will be entered by *data preparation* operators. Often a different preprinted form will be used for each different computer language.

coding standards See *programming standards.*

cold start The situation in which a program runs from the normal starting point, as if it had never been run before. Compare *warm start.*

collating Arranging in order; *e.g.* page 1, page 2, page 3, etc.

collating sequence Precedence with respect to one another, established for all characters in a character set.

collator A machine that collects sheets from different stacks to combine into new sets of paper. For example, 20 copies of 30 individual pages of a report are collected together to produce 20 reports of 30 pages.

color decoder An electronic device that converts coded *digital signals* into a form that can be used to add color to a monitor screen. Without such a device the screen would normally show two colors, usually black and white.

column binary Pertaining to *binary* representation of data on punched cards in which adjacent positions in a card column correspond to adjacent *bits* of data.

columnar working A facility provided by some word processing systems to manipulate information in columns.

.COM In the *CP/M* operating system, the d*extension* assigned to an object or binary file containing an executable program.

COM See *computer output microfilm.*

COMAL See *Common Algorithmic Language.*

comb printer A computer readout device using a set of characters mounted so as to face a paper sheet or roll.

command An instruction to the *disk operating system.*

command control language A program that controls some piece of equipment, especially in the military context. *JOVIAL* is described as a command and control language. Such programs are now more usually called *embedded systems.*

commercial data processing Data processing applications connected with business and commerce as compared to the processing of scientific and engineering applications.

Common Algorithmic Language (COMAL) A programming language developed initially for use in schools in Denmark, now used in the UK. It is defined as a set of extensions to *BASIC,* combining modern control constructs with the well known simplicity and familiarity of BASIC. It therefore facilitates the teaching of *structured programming* to beginners.

Common Business Oriented Language (COBOL) A programming language that was developed by *CODASYL* and is the de facto standard for *commercial data processing.* It first came into use during 1960.

common mode noise *Noise* that appears between both sides of a power line and ground.

communicating word processor (CWP) A word processor that has communication links via a switching system to common memory and printing devices. See also *dedicated word processor, shared logic system* and *standalone system.*

communication The action of transmitting or imparting information between people or machines.

communication information processor An information processor equipped with hardware/software to receive and transmit information from or to another computer system.

communication service The application of information technology in the telephone service and in information services handling specialist databases or access to *microfilm* records.

communication system A system supporting communication facilities such as voice services, *data transmission, audio conferencing* and *video conferencing.*

communications network A system of transmission pathways connecting communicating machines.

communications satellite An electronic device circling the earth that provides long distance *microwave communication* channels for voice services, data and broadcasts.

compact disk The application of *video disk* technology for the recording of audio signals coded as digital data. This provides higher recording densities and improved quality of reproduction.

compact interactive standard-COBOL (CIS-COBOL) A version of the programming language *COBOL* that runs on many of the popular *personal computers* above the hobby level. CIS-COBOL programs are portable between different *microcomputers,* thus making them useful for the development of program packages on the commercial market.

compatibility The ability to handle programs and data from one computer system without modification.

compatible (or IBM compatible) Able to run most IBM programs. (If a computer is able to run all IBM programs, it is said to be 100 percent IBM compatible.)

compile To prepare a machine language program from a symbolic language program by making use of the overall logic structure of the program.

compiler A program that translates *high level programming language* code into *low level programming language* code or *machine code.*

compiler diagnostics *Diagnostic messages* produced by a compiler.

compiler program See *compiler.*

complement See *one's complement, two's complement* and *ten's complement.*

composite symbol In flowcharting, a symbol made by adding to or combining shapes appearing on a flowcharting template.

computer A device or system that is capable of carrying out a sequence of operations in a distinctly and explicitly defined manner by automatically accepting and processing data. The computer may have a stored program or a *wired program.* See also *mainframe computer, minicomputer* and *microcomputer.*

computer aided/assisted design (CAD) The application of computer technology to the design of a product. It has been very successfully used to assist the detailed processes involved in designing electronic circuitry.

computer aided/assisted engineering (CAE) The collective term for systems that combine *CAD* with *CAM.*

computer aided/assisted instruction (CAI) The computer presents instructional text to the student, not recommended as an alternative to reading a book.

computer aided/assisted language learning (CALL) The computer is assisting with the development of skills in a foreign language.

computer aided/assisted learning (CAL) Computer aided or assisted learning helps a student to understand a subject by working with computer presented texts, simulations and questions.

computer aided/assisted manufacturing (CAM) A set of techniques that integrates all aspects of manufacturing systems within a factory, *i.e.* the use of computers for *process control, numerical control* of machine tools, automatic transfer systems such as guided pallets, *robotics* and the management aspects of automatic ordering of materials, predicting material usage, factory scheduling and inventory control. See also *computer aided/assisted design, computer aided/assisted engineering, computer integrated manufacturing, flexible machining system* and *flexible manufacturing system.*

computer aided/assisted testing (CAT) The computer presents the user with tests and records a score. See also *computer managed learning.*

computer aided/assisted training (CAT) See *computer based training.*

computer aided retrieval (CAR) The use of a computer to locate and display microfilmed documents quickly.

computer animation Computer generation of moving pictures.

computer architecture See *machine architecture.*

computer based learning (CBL) The computer provides materials for subject learning. See also *computer aided assisted learning.*

computer based message system (CBMS) An *electronic mail* service offered on an in-house network or rented from a public access network. An important advantage of a CBMS is a person to person message facility (rather than terminal to terminal). This is achieved by means of identity codes which a person must use to retrieve mail from the system.

computer based training (CBT) The computer presents materials for industrial or commercial training courses that can be taken by individuals whenever convenient.

computer bureaus See *bureau.*

computer conferencing (1) The ability for people at different physical locations to view information, *e.g.* a report or text document. (2) to read and record comments on a computer message system for later analysis. See also *audio conferencing* and *video conferencing.*

computer fiche See *microforms.*

computer generations The most significant developments in computer technology have been split into eras called generations. See also *first, second, third, fourth* and *fifth generation computers.*

computer graphics A mode of computer processing and output in which a significant part of the output information is in pictorial form. See also *graphics.*

computer input microfilm (CIM) Input devices that rely on *OCR* techniques to read character data or input processes that read data stored on special *microfilm* as binary code.

computer integrated manufacturing (CIM) The name given to the coordination of technology and computer applications that cover the following fuctions: business planning and support, engineering design, manufacturing planning, manufacturing control, technical floor monitoring and process automation. See also *computer aided/assisted design, computer aided/assisted manufacturing* and *numerical control.*

computer language See *programming language.*

computer mail See *electronic mail.*

computer managed instruction (CMI) The use of computers (usually off-line) to produce lesson requirements for an individual student based on previous results and test performance.

computer managed learning (CML) The computer software presents material to the user, directs progress to suitable sections and records the standards attained.

computer network A data network with computers at one or more of the *nodes.*

computer office system See *electronic office.*

computer operator The person who operates the computer, and where appropriate, responds to requests from the *operating system* and from remote users in a *time sharing* system.

computer output microfilm (COM) The process by which data is recorded on *microfilm* or *microfiche.* See also *computer integrated manufacturing.*

computer program See *program.*

computer science The study of computers, their underlying principles and use. It comprises such topics as: *programming; information* structures; *software engineering; programming languages; compilers* and *operating systems; hardware* design and testing; computer system architecture; computer *networks* and *interfacing; systems analysis* and design; theories of *information, systems* and computation; applicable mathematics and electronics; computing techniques *(e.g. graphics, simulation, artificial intelligence).*

computer system See *system.*

concatenation The production of long character *strings* by combining short ones.

concentrator A communication device that combines input lines whose total *bandwidth* is higher than that of the output line.

concurrency The operating system's ability to handle many tasks at the same time.

concurrent Running in parallel.

condition of transfer A machine *instruction* which discontinues the normal sequencing of machine instructions and orders a different instruction if certain programmed conditions occur.

conditional branch An *instruction* that may or may not cause a transfer from the normal sequence of instruction execution, depending upon the result of some operations.

conductor A medium that transmits (or conducts) energy. The energy could be in the form of heat or electricity.

conference call A service that enables three or more people to take part in one telephone conversation. See also *audio conferencing.*

Conference on Data Systems Languages (CODASYL) An organization of computing personnel from the computer industry, user organizations, software houses and other related groups that was founded at a meeting in the U.S.A. in 1959. Its aims were primarily to develop a standard data processing *programming language.* After a number of years it produced *COBOL.*

confidence level The probability that the true value of a parameter lies within a certain range of values.

configuration The particular hardware elements and their interconnection in a computer system for a particular period of operation.

console The workstation from which the operation of a computer system can be monitored and controlled.

console command processor (CCP) The *CP/M* command *interpreter* program.

console interpreter A *command* line parser and *interpreter* that executes system commands.

console printer A computer output *printer* used primarily for relaying information to the *operator.*

constant A value that does not change.

consumables The items associated with the use of equipment that wear out and need replacing, *e.g.* cassettes, disks, ribbons, or are used up by processing, *e.g.* paper.

contents addressable file store (CAFS) A method of organizing file storage in order to provide an efficient way of retrieving information by direct reference to the contents of the file rather than via indirect indexes.

continuous form paper One long continuous piece of paper divided by perforations into sheets and having on either side a tab containing *sprocket holes.*

control block A *data structure* set up to keep track of information related to a task in a *multiprogramming* environment.

control cards The *punch cards* containing the job control instructions that are added to the front of a card deck before processing can take place.

control character *ASCII* or *EBCDIC* characters used to control the input of data (*e.g.*, carriage return, line feed, XON).

control field A fixed portion of a data item or *record* where information for control purposes is placed. (Account numbers used in sequencing might be placed in a control field.)

control panel A part of the computer *console* that contains manual controls.

control program/monitor (CP/M) A commonly used *operating system* for *microcomputers* that are based on the Z80 *microprocessor chip.*

control statement Any programming *statement* that controls the sequence in which the program statements will be processed.

control table A *data structure* that contains information about a group of tasks or about physical *I/O* devices.

control total See *check total.*

control unit (CU) The portion of the *CPU* that contains the *instruction registers* and other elements that provide control over the movement of information between memory and the *arithmetic and logic unit* and hence the process of obeying program instructions.

controller A *hardware* circuit that controls access to a *peripheral* device such as a disk drive.

conversational mode A method of computer operation in which the user appears to be in continuous communication with the computer and receives immediate replies to input messages.

coprocessor An integrated *circuit* that can be coupled to a CPU *chip* to give it more abilities.

copy To produce a replica of some stored information.

The copy may be the duplication of a file on a disk, or a section of text in a word processed document. A copy process is often carried out as a *back-up* safeguard.

copyright The right to prevent copying. It is a negative right that can be exercised by a copyright owner if he or she chooses. Computer programs are considered to be protected under the law of copyright in a similar way to works of literature. This applies in most countries that have copyright legislation.

CORAL The name of a *high level programming language.*

core saturation The condition when an *inductor* or *transformer* core can no longer increase flux density.

core store A type of *non-volatile memory* in which binary information is stored in arrays of *ferrite cores.* Now it is more usual to find semiconductor memory.

core-image library A system *library* containing *machine-language* programs that are ready to be executed.

corporate database An information database holding data concerned with a specific company or organization.

correspondence management A component of the *electronic office,* it includes activities such as filing, indexing, document retrieval, document archiving, codes for filing and report facilities. See also *electronic filing.*

correspondence print quality A quality of printer output that is deemed acceptable for business correspondence. This usually means at least *daisy wheel printer* quality as compared to *line printer* or *dot matrix printer* output.

correspondence secretary An office worker who specializes in producing letters and other documents using word processing equipment.

corrupt To alter, deface or damage data so that it becomes inaccessible. This might be deliberate or accidental and caused by man or machine, *e.g.* manual alteration of data causing inconsistencies; physical damage by disk *read/write head* that prevents sections of data from being read.

corruption The deliberate or inadvertent destruction of computer information such that it is unreadable by any normal means or is no longer consistent. See also *corrupt* and *data integrity*.

cost benefit analysis A study to determine whether the benefits of recommended changes justify the cost.

counter A clocked digital electronic device that records the number of times a specific action takes place, *e.g.* a loop within a program, a binary counter in the computer *registers.*

courseware (1) The instructions that accompany a computer learning or training package. It may be part of the software or printed separately. (2) Training or learning materials in software form. See *computer aided/assisted instruction* and *computer aided/assisted learning.*

CPI See *characters per inch.*

CP/M See *control program/monitor.*

CPS See *characters per second.*

CPU See *Central processing unit.*

CR See *carriage return.*

crash A computer breakdown.

CRAY A series of high speed, powerful, scientific computers designed by Seymour Cray.

CRC See *cyclic redundancy check.*

CR/LF See *carriage return/line feed.*

credit card A card, usually plastic, that provides details of its owner's account with a credit agency. The details are provided on a magnetic strip that can be read by data *input devices* for automatic credit checking and debiting when the card is offered in payment for goods.

critical path See *network analysis.*

cross compiler A compiler for a *high level programming language* that runs on one machine producing code for a different machine.

crossfoot check The *system* check in which various results computed during processing are summed and compared to a total equal to their sum.

CRT See *cathode ray tube.*

cryogenic memory A type of memory operating at a very low temperature, usually that of liquid helium (about 4 degrees Kelvin). It uses the principles of superconductivity and electron tunneling. See also *Josephson memory.*

cryptography The protection of a message by either of two *encryption* methods, code or cipher. The first method involves a one to one substitution of a cipher text code for a plain text code using a codebook. The cipher process involves changing the plain text into cipher text by means of a cryptographic transformation using an algorithm or physical device to effect the transformation. See also *decryption.*

CSMA/CD See *carrier sense multiple access with collision detection.*

CTI Current task indicator. A single *byte* value that contains the number of currently active *tasks.*

CU See *control unit.*

cue See *prompt.*

current The movement of electrons through a *conductor.* It is measured in amperes.

cursor A symbol on a display screen that indicates the active position, *i.e.* the position at which the next character to be entered will be displayed. The symbol is often a small rectangle or the underline character and frequently it is made to blink or flash so that it can be easily distinguished within a screen of text.

cursor control keys A set of four or more keys for moving the *cursor* around the screen. Arrows indicating the direction of movement (up, down, left and right) are frequently marked.

cut and paste The action of selecting sections of text and moving them to another position within a document. When documents are prepared manually a draft would be physically cut up and pasted together in the correct sequence for retyping. With word processing software it is essential that a document is not physically adjusted but that any changes are marked on a printout with arrows indicating text movement.

cut-sheet paper feeder A *printer* attachment that automatically feeds paper in standard sheet sizes. It may be capable of also feeding envelopes.

CWP See *communicating word processor.*

cybernetics A discipline concerned with control and communciation in animal and machine. Cybernetics studies systems (electronic, organic or mechanical) that exhibit the characteristics of human behavior.

cycle time An interval of time in which one set of events or phenomena is completed. It is usually the time for one cycle of the memory system.

cyclic redundancy check (CRC) The most widely used error detecting check using a method of *check digit* control on blocks of data.

cycling tape When used by programmers, refers to making a new magnetic tape *file* by updating old magnetic tapes.

Cyclops system A system developed at the Open University to assist with communications between a tutor and one or more remote students. Handwritten or printed text and graphics can be transmitted from one Cyclops terminal to another via the public telephone network or can be recorded (and replayed) in sound coded form on an ordinary cassette recorder. The Cyclops TV screen can be used as a blackboard.

cylinder All *tracks* accessible at one setting of the *access mechanism* of a *direct access storage device.*

D

DAC See *digital to analog converter.*

daisy chain A series arrangement of functional units; *e.g.* a chain of disk drives connected together by cable with only the first drive in the chain connected to the peripheral *controller.*

daisy wheel printer A type of *serial printer* in which the *font* is formed on the ends of spokes of a rimless wheel (on the 'petals' of a daisy). The print quality is equal to that of a good typewriter and they are used with word processing systems for producing correspondence quality letters and documents.

DASD See *direct access storage device.*

data A general term for numbers, digits, characters and symbols that are accepted, stored and processed by a computer. When such data becomes meaningful to a person then the data components become *information.*

data administrator The coordinator of computer files and data bases who uses such aids as housekeeping routines and dictionaries.

data bank A collection of data bases or large files of data.

data base A collection of interrelated *data* stored so that it may be accessed by authorized users with simple *user-friendly* dialogs.

data base management A program that stores information in blocks of copy that may be arranged and rearranged as required.

data base management system (DBMS) An integrated software system that defines the logical and physical structure of data in a *data base* to facilitate and for accessing, entering and deleting data.

data buffer See *buffer.*

data capture The action involved in collecting data for use in a particular computer process. It may be done automatically, *e.g.* the continuous monitoring of temperature in a chemical process, or manually as in gas meter reading.

data cartridge See *cartridge.*

data cell drive A *direct-access storage device* capable of holding large amounts of data on removable data *cells* which are the data-recording medium.

data channel An information route and associated circuitry that is used for the transfer of data between systems or parts of systems. See also *channel.*

data collection The process of collecting data from a point where it has been captured or entered as a separate process. Generally the equipment is connected to the host computer but in some applications portable equipment is carried to different areas for information to be entered, *e.g.* portable bar code reader. The stored information is either transmitted to the host computer directly or via portable storage devices such as magnetic tape *cartridges.*

data communications The transmission of *data* or *information* from one computer to another.

data communications equipment (DCE) The side of an interface that represents the provider of a data communication facility in a standard such as *RS232C* or *X.25.* DCEs are usually analog or digital *modems.* Compare *data terminal equipment.*

data concentrator See *network processor.*

data control A manual activity, more usually associated with *batch* systems, where large quantities of data for computer processing are collected, checked and organized for either *data preparation* or direct processing.

data description language (DDL) The section of a data base system that is concerned with the description of the logical data structure.

data dictionary/directory (DD/D) A structured description of a data base. A data dictionary will contain descriptions of and relations between the data *entities,* including any details of validation and authorization for access. A data directory holds details of the physical mapping of the logical data onto the physical storage structures.

data disk (file disk, working disk) The *disk* on which a user stores *files.*

data encryption See *encryption.*

data engineering See *telematics.*

data entry The process by which an operator uses a keyboard or other input device to enter data directly into a computer system. Compare *data capture* and *data preparation.*

data file A file containing data as opposed to a program and to text.

data integrity A measure of the reliability of data used by a specific computer system. A high level of data integrity is possible if both hardware and software errors are avoided, *e.g.* magnetic storage equipment is chosen for its reliability and data transfer processes have software checks that will quickly identify any error.

data link A physical connection between two or more devices by a communication channel, *e.g.* telephone lines, *coaxial cables, optical fibers.*

data logging The automatic collection of data by a machine. This can refer to the external collection of physical data for later use by a computer or the internal logging of processes being carried out by a computer.

data management A term normally used to refer to systems that offer a user *interface* whereby the details of the physical handling of the files is dealt with automatically, leaving users free to concentrate on the logical properties of the data.

data manipulation language (DML) The facilities of a *data base management system* concerned with the storage, access and amendment of data. In the case of *relational data base* systems this facility is more usually provided as a *query language.*

data medium Any material having a property that enables data to be represented—either by a two state binary code such as magnetic tape and disks or as alphanumeric characters such as printer paper or a VDU screen.

data network A communications network that is devoted to carrying computer information as opposed to voice, video, etc.

data preparation The process of translating data into a suitable machine readable form. In the past data has been transferred to *paper tape, punched cards* and magnetic tape for later input to a computer. Now it is much more usual to use direct *data entry* and *data capture* processing.

data processing (DP) The operation of collecting, storing, processing and transmitting data. The term can be used to refer to a class of computer applications or a function within an organization.

data protection legislation Legislation aimed at controlling the misuse of personal data handled in computers. The unauthorized transfer of electronic data can constitute an infringement of personal privacy. Safeguards are required to declare and/or register the use for which data is stored.

data retrieval The process of searching for and selecting data from some area of storage linked to a computer.

data signals A means of transmitting data using either *analog* or *digital* signals.

data sink The point of receipt of data in a data communication system.

data source The point of origin for data in a data communication system.

data structure A particular arrangement of information in which the contents, the organizational relations among the components, and the permissible operations are constrained by a set of rules peculiar to that data structure, *i.e.* arrays and linked lists.

data structure diagram (DSD) A diagram that describes the logical structure of the data in terms of *entities, records, attributes* and logical *pointers* between items of data.

data tablet A graphical input device that can generate digital signals that represent the movement of a pen or pencil over a flat surface.

data terminal equipment (DTE) The side of an interface that represents the user of a data communication facility, in a standard such as *RS232C* or *X.25.* DTEs are usually computers or computer terminals. Compare *data communications equipment.*

data transfer rate The rate at which data can be moved between devices. This can be constrained by the speed of the read/write device or the capability of the transmission link. *Buffers* are used to interface devices with different speed characteristics.

data translation The process of converting data from the form used by one system to that required by another.

data transmission The process of sending data *(analog* or *digital* measurements, coded characters, or information in general) from a sender to one or more receivers.

data type The definition of a specific data form that matches a well defined class of items, *e.g. real number, integer number, string.*

data validation See *validation.*

data word A *word* that can only, or is expected only to contain data.

dataflow diagram (DFD) A diagram that describes the flow of information for a specific process or application.

DBMS See *Data base management system.*

DBS See *direct broadcasting by satellite.*

DC See *direct current.*

DCE See *data communications equipment.*

DDCMP See *digital data communication message protocol.*

DD/D Data dictionary/directory. A collection of data that functions as a combined catalog, dictionary and directory—describing and locating each data element.

DDE Direct data entry. See *data entry.*

DDL See *data description language.*

deadlock See *deadly embrace.*

deadly embrace A situation that may arise when two or more processes are competing for available resources. For example, one task requires terminal input and the use of the printer and has acquired the terminal link; but before it can link up to the printer and complete the process, a second task has linked into the printer but requires the terminal for an input sequence. In this case neither task can obtain its required resources in order to complete processing.

debit card terminal See *automatic teller machines.*

debug To find and remove errors or *bugs* from a program or system.

decentralization Organizing support services, such as word or data processing, to support specific users.

decentralized system A system in which equipment is located near where the work originates, rather than in one central location.

decibel A measurement of the intensity of loudness of sound.

decimal number system A numeration system having a *base* of 10 and using the digits 0, 1, 2, 3, 4, 5, 6, 7, 8 and 9.

decimal tab A key on word processing equipment for entering numbers. It automatically moves the *cursor* to the decimal point and the cursor then moves from right to left until the 'point key' is pressed.

decision support system (DSS) An information processing system that extends assistance to senior managers in the area of strategic planning. It can include tools to interact with current and historical data bases and provide underlying trends, enabling projections and the outcome of hypothetical courses of action to be examined.

decision table A table showing the relationship between named *variables* and specifying actions to be taken when specific conditions arise.

decoder The means by which *decoding* takes place. This can be carried out by hardware or software.

decoding The action of transferring data from its encoded form back to its original state. See also *encoding.*

decollator A machine which separates the continuous strings of sheets of multipart forms.

decryption The transformation of encrypted data back into its original form. Compare *encryption.*

dedicated computer A computer committed entirely to a single task, *e.g.* controlling a pumping station.

dedicated line A separate electrical or communications line reserved for use by a particular machine or company.

dedicated word processor A computer designed mainly for processing text.

default A processing action that is built into a program for use when an explicit specification for that action is not supplied by the user.

default response The simple user response, *e.g.* pressing the return key, which will enter a *default value* for a data item.

default value This is the value that will be taken automatically by the computer in the event of the omission of an entry item.

Defense Advanced Research Projects Agency (DARPA) An agency of the U.S. Department of Defense responsible for research and technical development in areas where no single service (Army, Navy, Air Force, Marine Corps) has a clear jurisdiction or interest. It is most famous for the network technology development that led to the *ARPANET*.

delete To remove or eliminate, *e.g.* delete data from a file.

delimiter A *character* used to mark the end of one part of a *command* or *program statement* and the start of the next.

delta A standard three-phase connection with the ends of each phase winding connected in series to form a closed loop with each phase 120 degrees from the other. Sometimes referred to as a three-wire.

delta-delta The connections between a *delta* source and a *delta* load.

delta-wye A term or symbol indicating the primary connected in *delta* and the secondary in *wye* when pertaining to a three-phase *transformer* or transformer bank.

demultiplexer A unit that divides one or more information *streams* into a larger number of streams.

denary notation The normal numbering system using a base of 10, *i.e.* using the digits 0 to 9.

density The compactness of information stored on a diskette. A diskette can have single, double, or quadruple density.

density of a storage medium A measure of the amount of information that can be held on a specific dimension of the medium. For magnetic tape it is the number of bits per unit length of tape, for a magnetic disk it is the number of bits per *sector,* number of sectors per *track* and tracks per disk.

descender The part of a letter that appears below a baseline, *e.g.* letters *q, p, y, g, j* have descenders.

desk check See *dry run.*

desktop computer A compter small enough to fit on a desk, typically a compact unit with *screen, keyboard* and *disk storage* combined.

desktop publishing The production of professional-quality published materials by means of a desktop microcomputer and a high-resolution printer. Desktop publishing is often used for in-house publications, such as newsletters.

development disk A powerful microcomputer system that may have either *tape* or *disk* storage, a moderate amount of main *memory,* and several *peripheral* interfaces. A development disk often is used to create new software for specialized *applications.*

device A piece of equipment.

device assignments Logical-to-physical assignments that allow *peripheral* devices to be traded as needed for an *application* without having to be physically disconnected and reconnected.

DFD See *Dataflow diagram.*

diagnostic message A message that gives details about a processing failure, *e.g.* error, or the current state of processing, *e.g.* sorting.

diagnostic routine A routine within a program that is entered as a result of some error condition having been detected. It attempts to analyze the fault and provide appropriate action/*diagnostic messages,* recording any values that might be useful in tracing the cause of an error.

diary management A component of the *electronic office,* facilities include recording and retrieving appointment details, obtaining holiday and absence checklists and in some cases keeping schedules of room use.

dictionary Any data structure representing a set of elements that can support the insertion and deletion of elements as well as test for membership. See also *data dictionary.*

digipad An *input* device on which freehand drawing is translated into digitized form. The resulting image is displayed on a *VDU* screen and can be stored.

digital Using discrete, electronic, on/off (one or zero) impulses to represent information.

digital computer A computer that operates on discrete quantities. It works with data represented in a digital form, usually the binary 0s and 1s. Compare *analog computer.*

digital data communication message protocol (DDCMP) A data link control *protocol* developed by the Digital Equipment Corporation (DEC). It is similar to *SDLC* and *HDLC* but is character oriented rather than bit oriented.

digital exchange A telephone or data switching station that uses digital technology.

digital information Information held in *digital* form, convenient to transmit, analyze and subsequently transfer back to the original form, *e.g.* pictures, medical scanners, music, financial information, text, business data.

digital network A network designed to interconnect computers handling *digital information.* See also *network* and *communication system.*

digital signal A waveform or signal whose *voltage* at any particular time will be at any one of a group of discrete levels, generally two. A two level signal is sometimes called a binary digital signal or binary signal and corresponds to the two binary states logic 1 (TRUE) and logic 0 (FALSE). Compare *analog signal.*

digital signal processing The branch of *signal processing* that uses digital systems to operate on signals. The advantages of digital over analog signal processing include: better use of memory, a wider range of arithmetic operations and higher possible precision.

digital switchboard A telephone switchboard with a *digital computer* to provide facilities such as call *queueing,* diverting unanswered calls to other extensions, the use of different ringing tones to distinguish internal and external callers and a memory store for numbers that are used frequently.

digital switching The switching of communication lines via *digital signal* controls rather than the older *analog signal* transmission network.

digital to analog converter (DAC) A device that can accept a *digital signal* and produce an equivalent analog signal. Compare *ADC.*

digitizer A device that converts *analog signals* into digits, *i.e.* an *A/D converter.*

digitrons A fluorescent gas discharge display, used to display data on a screen. Digitrons require a fairly high voltage as well as additional circuitry which increases their cost above *LEDs.* However these fluorescent displays are larger and clearer than LEDs and are usually green although yellow and orange displays are also in use. See also *LCD.*

DIL See *dual in-line package.*

dimension of an array The number of *subscripts* needed to locate any *element* in the *array.*

diode An electronic device, generally of semiconductor material, that has two terminals and is capable of allowing current flow in one direction only. The terminals are called the anode and cathode.

diode transistor logic (DTL) An early form of logic family, normally produced in *integrated circuit* form, whose principle switching components consist of semiconductor *diodes* and *transistors.*

DIP See *dual in-line package.*

direct access processing A technique of handling data in random order without preliminary sorting, utilizing files on *direct-access storage* disks.

direct access storage device (DASD) One of a class of storage devices that can access storage locations in any order; a sequential search is not required and the access time to read and write to a particular location is relatively independent of the position of the last location accessed. See also *random access.*

direct addressing The 'normal' mode of addressing in which the *address* specified in a computer instruction is the machine address to be used.

direct broadcasting by satellite (DBS) Modern satellites have enough power and new antennae so that broadcasts can be transmitted directly to some specific part of the earth's surface.

direct changeover The introduction of a completely new system without any reference or *parallel running* with a previous system.

direct current (DC) An essentially consistent value current that flows in only one direction. Compare *alternating current.*

direct data entry (DDE) See *data entry.*

Direct Information Access Network in Europe (DIANE) The information available through this network is aimed at researchers, engineers, scientists, managers, economists, the legal and medical professions. *Euronet*-DIANE is a private network and users need to subscribe to the service.

direct memory access (DMA) A method whereby *I/O* processes can obtain access to the *CPU's* memory while a program is running.

directory A list of the *files* that are stored on an individual disk.

disassembler A program that translates from *machine code* to an *assembly language,* generally used to decipher existing machine code by generating the equivalent symbolic codes. It provides an aid for *debugging.*

disc See *Floppy disk.*

discrete media Storage media, such as diskettes and magnetic tape, that are not a fixture of the system and can be removed at will.

discretionary hyphen A *hyphen* that is inserted within a word to improve the appearance of text. A discretionary hyphen is not permanent; if the length of the line is changed, the hyphen may be automatically dropped by the system. See also *rehyphenation* and *required hyphen.*

disk drive A peripheral device with *read/write heads* and associated electronics that can store and retrieve data from disks.

disk file A set of related records held on a *storage disk.*

disk operating system (DOS) (pronounced DAHSS) An acronym for *disk operating system,* the program that controls a computer's basic functions, such as printing documents and processing data software programs. Different computers use different operating systems.

disk pack An assembly of several rigid disks that are equally spaced on a central spindle and treated as a single storage unit for mounting on a *disk drive.*

disk storage *Backing store* that uses disks.

disk-based micro system A *microcomputer* system with magnetic disk *backing store.*

display See *video display unit.*

display format The amount of characters that can fit onto a screen, described as either a number of lines and characters per line or the total number of characters.

display screen See *video display unit.*

distributed data base system A database in which the data is contained within a number of separate subsystems, usually at different physical locations.

distributed file system A simple version of a *distributed data base system* in which individual files may be accessed at *remote* sites but where sites do not have facilities to process queries involving cross-file connection.

distributed logic A *shared-resource system* in which the *microprocessors* that control most text-editing and printing operations are contained in the individual *workstations* and *printers.*

distributed network A loosely coupled *network* of computers communicating over some form of *data-communications* link either *synchronously* or *asynchronously.*

distributed processing The organization of processing to be carried out on a *distributed system.* Each computer is free to process local data and make local decisions. The computers exchange information with each other over a data communication network in order to process data or to read decisions that affect multiple processes. Compare *centralized data processing.*

distributed system Any system in which a number of independent interconnected computers can contribute.

distribution network See *local area network* and *wide area network.*

distributor A broker in the information processing business who buys products from a manufacturer and passes them on to dealers.

DML (data manipulation language) A language that permits the user to interact with the data base through statements that occur in everyday speech.

document A portion of text treated by an information processing system as one complete unit, usually associated with a unique file name.

document assembly The word processing procedure for collating separate sections of text, such as paragraphs, to form a new complete document.

document cycle The stages through which a document passes from conception to final destination. The stages include origination, processing, revision, reproduction, distribution, and filing/storing.

document format The set-up, layout, or design of a document (including margins, tabs, etc.).

document merging A facility to merge documents or text from two sources using word processing software.

document processing The machine processing (reading, sorting, collating, etc.) of documents that are generally readable by people and machines, *e.g.* bank checks, *turnaround documents* from public utility companies.

document protection The ability to protect documents from unauthorized access by the use of *passwords.*

document reader A machine for reading documents that are encoded in a way that is readable by person and machine. See also *mark sense reader, optical mark reading.*

document recovery The facility, on some word processors, to reestablish a document that has been accidentally deleted.

document storage/retrieval The use of computer facilities, dedicated word processors or otherwise, to store and retrieve documents and text.

documentation All material that describes a system and makes that system more easily used or understood. Documentation is frequently classified according to its purpose; thus there may be design documents, specification documents, programming documents and user documents.

domestic applications The use of information technology in the home. See also *wired household.*

dopants The selected impurities that are added to purified silicon enabling the modified material to conduct a current, *e.g.* boron for positive conductivity and phosphorous for negative conductivity. See also *n-type material* and *p-type material.*

doped semiconductor A semiconductor material that has had a specific impurity added to adjust its electrical properties, *i.e.* the addition of a *dopant.*

DOS See *disk operating system.*

dot matrix printer A *printer* where characters are formed of ink dots from a rectangluar matrix of printing positions, typically 9 × 7. It may be a *serial printer* or a *line printer.*

double buffering A form of buffering in which two *buffers* are used, *e.g.* two output buffers that interchange: first, one is used by the program for holding output for a printer while the other is being read and emptied by the printer, then they exchange roles.

double length word A hardware feature of many computers where two words (*e.g.* 16 bits) can be joined together and manipulated as a single (32 bit) word in the *central processor.*

download To transfer data from a *mainframe* or other large computer storage facility to a smaller unit, *e.g. microcomputer.* The process may use telephone lines, radio or television communications.

downtime The time during which the equipment or computer system was not available for use.

DP See *data processing.*

drive The device that moves the disk past the *read/write head* in a microcomputer.

driver (1) A routine within an operating system that handles the individual peripheral units on a computer system. (2) Also an electronic circuit that is capable of providing large currents or voltages to other circuits connected to the driver's output.

drum plotter A *plotter* suitable for very large drawings where the paper is wrapped around the drum, with take-up spools on either side. The pen can move along a track across the width of the drum to provide one axis and the paper moves to provide the second axis of the two dimensional picture. See also *x-y plotter.*

drum printer A type of impace *line printer* in which the *font* (characters and timing marks) is etched on a steel band. Speeds vary from 300 to 2500 lines per minute.

drum storage See *magnetic drum.*

dry run The use of *test data* to check the paths through a program or *flowchart* without the use of a computer.

DSD See *data structure diagram.*

DSS See *decision support system.*

DTE See *data terminal equipment.*

DTL See *diode transistor logic.*

dual in-line package (DIL and DIP) A circuit that is fabricated on a single *silicon chip* and is encapsulated in such a way that the external connections are made accessible by means of two parallel rows of terminating pins perpendicular to the edges of the package.

dual processor A multiprocessor system with two *central processors.* In some cases the second processor is redundant until there is a failure in the first processor, *i.e.* provides system back-up facilities.

dual station This facility enables two *VDUs* to access one *word processing unit.*

dumb terminal A terminal that has no independent processing capability. It is generally used as a peripheral to a *mainframe* or *minicomputer* system. Compare *intelligent terminal.*

dummy variable An *identifier* used for *syntax* reasons in a program, but which will be replaced by some other variable identifier when the program is executed; a common example is the use of a dummy variable in the definition of a *subprogram* parameter.

dump A word used to describe the process of copying the data in a section of memory and sending it to a peripheral device. This output, known as a dump, may be used to ensure the integrity of data in a file (*back-up*), or to assist in program error detection.

dumping The action of obtaining a *dump.*

duplex A form of serial data collection in which transmission may occur in both directions. See *full duplex, half duplex* and *simplex operation.*

duplexing Printing on both sides of the paper.

duplicate To make a copy of an item such as a file or disk.

dust control Aspects of computer environmental control that can require air conditioning, special carpets and dust mats in a geographical location with a high atmospheric pollution, *i.e.* industrial areas.

dynamic data structure A data structure whose organizational characteristics may change during its lifetime. Its increased adaptability is often at the expense of decreased efficiency in accessing *elements* of the structure.

dynamic memory A form of *volatile* semiconductor memory, *e.g., RAM*, in which data must be refreshed, *i.e.,* read and rewritten, periodically (approximately every 2 milliseconds).

dynamic RAM See *dynamic memory.*

dynamic relocation The movement of part or all of a currently executing program from one area of storage to another.

dynamic stop A program stop that performs an infinite loop until an operator action takes place allowing the process to continue.

dynamic storage Storage assigned to data values on demand while a program is executing.

E

EAPROM See *electrically alterable programmable read only memory.*

EAROM See *electrically alterable read only memory.*

earth station A microwave relay station which transmits information between a *communications satellite* and other communications systems.

EBCDIC See *extended binary-coded decimal interchange code.*

echo The reflection of transmitted data back to its source, *e.g.* characters typed on a keyboard will not appear unless they are echoed. See also *duplex operation.*

ECL See *emitter coupled logic.*

ECONET A trade name for a *local area network* designed by Acorn Computers for the BBC microcomputer.

edge connector A socket whose contacts are arranged according to a standard pattern. The socket is capable of accepting a standard-sized *circuit board* having contact areas that are formed along its edge and can mate with the corresponding contacts in the socket.

edit To change text in some way, such as by correcting, revising, reformatting, or rearranging.

editor A program used to create or modify *files* under human control.

EDP Electronic data processing. See *data processing.*

EDSAC Electronic Delay Storage Automatic Computer (1949).

EDVAC Electrical Discrete Variable Automatic Computer (1949).

EEROM See *electrically erasable read only memory.*

effective address An *address* derived after performing any specified address determination activity.

EFTS See *electronic funds transfer system.*

EHF See *extremely high frequency.*

EIA Electronics Industries Association.

eighty-column card See *punched card.*

electrically alterable programmable read only memory (EAPROM) The programmable version of the *EAROM.* See also *programmable read only memory.*

electrically alterable read only memory (EAROM) A form of semiconductor memory in which it is possible to change the contents of selected memory locations by applying suitable electrical signals. Normally these changes are infrequent and the device is essentially a *ROM,* not a *RAM.*

electrically erasable read only memory (EEROM) A form of semiconductor memory in which the entire contents can be erased by subjecting the device to suitable electrical signals. After the contents have been erased, the device may be reprogrammed.

electromagnetic radiation The energy waves that are radiated from a transmitting aerial. Electromagnetic waves have properties similar to light waves but of lower frequency.

electronic data processing (EDP) See *data processing.*

electronic diaries See *diary management.*

electronic filing A computer based system for the storage, cataloging and retrieval of documents. A comprehensive system should give a high degree of security both against computer failure and against unauthorized access, together with a flexible method of organizing its components. See also *correspondence management, electronic office* and *microfilm.*

electronic funds transfer system (EFTS) The general use of computers in effecting payments between individuals and/or organizations, *e.g.* long established check clearance by banks. In some cases the term is used to refer to advanced systems in which debits and credits are made simultaneously as a transaction takes place, *e.g.* immediate credit card payment in a supermarket with special card readers.

Electronic Industries Association (EIA) This association is composed of manufacturers of electronic equipment in the U.S.A. who are concerned with lobbying for the development and manufacture of electronic equipment.

electronic keyboard A typing machine that acts by interpreting electrical signals. The signals are generated when key depression causes closure of two electrical contacts.

electronic mail (1) Messages sent from one user of a computer system to one or more recipients using electronic communication and storage techniques. *Multimedia mail* can combine text, *graphics,* voice, *facsimile transmission* and other forms of information in a single message. Other functions often performed by an electronic mail system include checking a user's identity, expanding named mailing lists into lists of recipients and interrogating directory services to locate a user for which only partial details are known. (2) The facility to store electronic mail for subsequent forwarding to the recipient.

electronic messaging Using a software package which can be installed in a *local area network* to provide an internal electronic mail facility.

electronic money Any electronic device that can be used instead of money for payment of goods and services, *e.g. credit cards, phonecards.*

electronic office An office environment supported by *integrated office automation* systems. A full office automation system totally integrates word processing, management communications and advanced text management with data processing. Such systems provide networking capability to support both management and administrative workstations and feature: *word processing, advanced text management, electronic mail, management support, management information systems, correspondence management* and *data processing* applications.

electronic payment service See *electronic funds transfer system.*

electronic publishing The replacement of the traditional means of printing, storing and disseminating of paper by the equivalent operations on electronic messages, e.g. the development of material via a word processor for later computer typesetting.

Electronic Random Number Indicator Equipment (ERNIE) See *random numbers.*

electronic shopping The development of home shopping and mail order systems such as providing catalogs on video cassettes or disks and using a two-way communication system for orders, quoting credit card numbers for payment.

electronic signature A special encoding technique such that data or messages that have been generated using special codes prior to transmission are decoded to indicate the identity of the sender precisely, *i.e.* the information bears an electronic signature.

electronic spreadsheet An electronic calculating tool which allows numeric data to be displayed in a variety of formats. It is commonly used for preparing budgets, comparing proposals, evaluating alternatives and making forecasts.

electronic typewriter (ELT) There are four categories: (1) This category includes a basic machine with electronic keyboard, *daisy wheel printer,* choice of pitch and automatic correction from a small *buffer* memory. The buffer may vary from 15 characters to one line of type. The basic ELT has no internal/permanent memory. (2) This category has 2 or 3 line correction buffers, permanent memories up to 4000 characters, plus automatic centering, underlining and other features. (3) This category has internal/permanent memories in excess of 4000 characters. Some of these ELTs do not have visual displays but include a wide range of automatic features such as editing and storage facilities. (4) Machines in this category have varied features, including unlimited external memories, *e.g.* removable disks. They can usually be upgraded to provide word processing workstations.

electrophotographic printer A printer that uses the same principle as that used by many office copiers. In a copier the light image is a projection of the original document via a lens system, while in a printer the image is formed by a modulated light beam from a laser, the face of a display tube or an array of light emitting diodes.

The required image is written by a beam of light onto a photoconductive drum or band that has a uniform electric charge over its surface. The action of the light beam causes local conductivity and allows the surface to assume the potential of the substrate. The charge pattern is then developed by applying particles of pigment that carry an appropriate electrostatic charge.

electrosensitive printing Printing that requires specially coated paper which can be sensitized to produce an image. This type of printing is generally quiet in operation but produces a relatively low print quality.

electrostatic printer A type of printer in which the required image is first written as a pattern of electrostatic charge, and is made visible by bringing the pattern in contact with particles of pigment that carry a charge of opposite polarity. The term electrostatic printer is often used to refer to all printers in which an electrostatic image is used as part of the print process, including *electrophotographic printers.*

element A component of a larger group or set.

ELF See *extremely low frequency.*

elite type A *typeface* with a printing *pitch* of 12 characters to the horizontal inch.

ELT See *electronic typewriter.*

embedded command These commands are inserted into text in order to define the *format* for a finished document. They are visible when editing but take effect when a document is previewed on the screen or printed. Typical commands include: setting margins, *justification, indentation,* page and line length, predefined *headings* and *footings,* line spacing and control codes for different *print styles.*

embedded system Any system that uses a computer as a component, but whose prime function is not that of a computer, *e.g.* guided weapons system, blood analyzer.

emboldening Choosing a word processing option to print text in bold type.

emitter coupled logic (ECL) A high-speed logic family available in the form of integrated circuits based on *bipolar transistors.* The fast switching speeds are achieved by means of a design that avoids driving the transistors into saturation.

emulation The exact execution on a given computer of a program written for a different computer, accepting identical data and producing identical results. This is usually accomplished by means of hardware that enables software originally written for another computer to be used without being rewritten.

emulator Any system that permits the process of *emulation* to be carried out.

encoder Any hardware or software system that provides a method of transferring information from its original form, *e.g.* characters and numbers, into a different form. The form might be a code that is simpler to handle, a binary number for internal use by a computer or an encrypted value for security purposes.

encoding The transformation of a message into an encoded form. See also *encoder.*

encoding information See *encoder.*

encryption The transformation of plain text to a cipher text by means of cryptographic transformation and an associated key or by means of a codebook. It's purpose usually is to make the data meaningless to those who do not know the necessary keys for decryption. See also *cryptography.*

end mark A marker placed at the end of a stream of data.

End of Block (EOB) Indicating the end of a block of text (word processing) or data (magnetic storage media).

End of Data (EOD) A code that is written into a serially accessed memory such as magnetic tape. It indicates the starting point for new records.

End of File (EOF) A marker indicating the end of a file.

End of Job (EOJ) A marker indicating the end of a job, usually used in batch streams.

End of Record (EOR) A marker indicating the end of a record, usually needed for free format records stored sequentially.

End of Tape (EOT) A marker used to indicate the end of a magnetic tape to the *tape transport* mechanism. Compare *BOT* marker.

endless loop magnetic tape The recording media used in many centralized dictation systems. The tape moves in a never-ending loop.

end-user The equipment or computer user who is concerned with using a specific application linked to work requirements.

end-user language A language providing facilities to create programs using commands and procedures that are natural to the users, who may be unaware they are generating programs.

enhanced matrix A means of producing a better than usual dot matrix print output by overlapping the dots.

enhancement An extra facility added to a process or piece of equipment.

ENIAC Electronic Numerical Integrator and Calculator (1946).

entity An item type providing record entries in a file or data base, *e.g.* stock item, staff member, customer. See also *attribute.*

enumerative data type A programmer defined data type in which each *value* is drawn from a finite repertoire of discrete, mutually exclusive values.

envelope Describes how a musical note varies while it is sounding. *Microcomputers* offering 'music' facilities use envelope controls to permit sound pitch and intensity to be controlled.

EOB See *End of Block.*

EOD See *End of Data.*

EOF See *End of File.*

EOJ See *End of Job.*

EOL End of line. A special signal (*character*) that is placed after the final character of information on a line.

EOR See *End of Record.*

EOT See *End of Tape.*

epitaxy A method of forming a thin layer of material, *i.e.* a *wafer,* on a base allowing materials other than silicon to be used for making *chips.*

EPROM See *erasable programmable read only memory.*

equivalence function See *exclusive NOR function.*

equivalence gate See *exclusive NOR gate.*

erasable programmable read only memory (EPROM) A type of *PROM* that is capable of being programmed a number of times by the user. The contents of EPROMs are generally erased by exposure to hard ultraviolet radiation.

erasable store A storage medium that can be used repeatedly as new data overwrites the old data, *e.g.* magnetic tape and disks.

erase The rubbing out of data that has been stored. It necessitates the data being replaced by a code that means null data such as zeros.

ergonomics The analysis of how people, machines and equipment work together.

ERNIE See *Electronic Random Number Indicator Equipment.*

error The situation when the results of a process are not as expected. For example, a hardware error will occur when equipment becomes faulty and software errors occur when programs do not perform correctly.

error detection The cause of an error is found by looking at any diagnostics that identify the location of a fault. *Trace* facilities can be used if the reason for an incorrect processing result cannot be linked with a specific coding mistake/equipment malfunction. See also *check digit* and *parity bit.*

error message A diagnostic message that is printed or displayed to help identify the cause of a problem.

escape sequence A set of *format controls* created from multiple *characters,* with the first character being the Escape Signal Code, decimal 27.

E-time Execution time. The time required to perform the operation specified by an instruction.

evaluation In the execution of a program, the process of finding the value of an expression.

EVFU Electronic vertical format unit.

exchange See *digital exchange.*

exchangeable disk A disk or *disk pack* that can be removed from the disk unit for storage or later use by the same computer or another compatible machine. See also *fixed disk.*

exchangeable disk pack See *exchangeable disk.*

exclusive NOR function (EXNOR) This function combines statements such that the outcome is true (1) when all the statements are true (1) or when all the statements are false (0), otherwise the outcome is false (0). It is also referred to as an equivalence function.

exclusive NOR gate (EXNOR) An electronic logic gate that performs according to the *exclusive NOR function*, *i.e.* the output is (1) when all input values are (1) or when all input values are (0). It is also referred to as an equivalence gate.

exclusive OR function (EXOR) This function combines statements such that the outcome is false (0) when all statements are true (1) or when all statements are false (0), otherwise the outcome is true (1). It is also referred to as a nonequivalence function.

exclusive OR gate (EXOR) An electronic logic gate that performs according to the *exclusive OR function, i.e.* the output is (0) when all input values are (1) or when all input values are (0). It is also referred to as a nonequivalence gate.

execution error See *run time error.*

execution phase The time during a program run in which the program is actually being executed or the part of a process cycle when an instruction is being obeyed.

executive program Originally the control program that schedules the use of the hardware required by the program being run. Also called supervisor program or monitor. In modern, more complex, systems an executive is responsible for the supervision of many disjoint processes.

executive terminal A workstation designed specially for managerial tasks.

exit To transfer control from a subprogram back to the calling program (return statement) or from the program entirely (stop statement).

exit point The point at which control leaves a subroutine.

EXNOR See *exclusive NOR.*

EXOR See *exclusive OR.*

expert system A software package aimed at providing expert 'consultancy' advice and assistance with problem solving in limited specialist fields of science, engineering, mathematics, medicine and education, etc.

exponent See *floating point notation.*

exponentiation The operation of raising to a power, *e.g.* 2 raised to the power 3 is 2^3.

expression In a programming language, a sequence of *constants, variable* names, and function names connected by operator symbols.

extended binary-coded decimal interchange code (EBCDIC) An 8 bit character encoding scheme primarily used on the IBM 360-370 series of computers.

extension A code (usually a period and three letters) added to a *file name* for identification purposes. For example, each file having to do with customer service has the code .CUS at the end of the file name.

extent A dummy file *control block* used to end the size of a disk *file.*

external data transfer The movement of *data* to or from *main storage.*

external storage Any type of storage device that is connected to and controlled by a computer but is not integrated within it, *e.g.* magnetic disk, magnetic tape. An external storage device may be shared between computers.

extremely high frequency (EHF) A band of radio frequencies between 30GHz and 300GHz, used for millimeter wave systems.

extremely low frequency (ELF) A band of radio frequencies below 300Hz.

F

facsimile transmission (FAX) Systems that provide electronic transmission of ordinary documents, including drawings, photographs and maps. The original document is scanned and converted into *analog* or *digital* signals for transmission.

fail safe The ability of a piece of equipment to correctly terminate processing or its activity when a fault occurs.

fail soft The ability of a computer system to provide a reduced level of service in spite of the occurrence of a single fault. See also *fault tolerant system.*

fanfold paper Continuous lengths of computer paper, perforated at regular intervals and folded in the manner of a fan for easy storage and use.

fan-in The number of input lines to a *logic gate* or logic device.

fan-out The maximum number of devices that can be safely driven by the output from a *logic gate* or logic device. If the fan-out is exceeded, then the voltage levels corresponding to the logic 1 and logic 0 states become more similar and errors are more likely.

fast core A type of core store that has a lower access time than the devices used for working store in the same processor.

fast line A telecommunications line that is capable of transmitting data at a 48K or 96K *baud rate*.

father file See *ancestral file system.*

fault detection The determination of errors in a logic circuit, arithmetic circuit or during an information transfer. The error is detected by some type of automatic check within the hardware or software.

fault diagnosis The task of identifying the cause of a fault.

fault tolerant system A computer system that is capable of providing either full functionality or reduced functionality after a failure has occurred. Fault tolerance is usually provided through a combination of redundant system elements and error detection and correction procedures.

FAX See *facsimile transmission.*

FCB File control block. A block of data used to hold the name and physical attributes of a disk file. Usually stored on disk in a directory of files, the file control block is copied to memory when the file is in use.

FCC See *Federal Communications Commission.*

feasibility study A study carried out prior to a development project in order to establish that the proposed system is feasible and can serve a useful purpose.

Federal Communications Commission (FCC) The U.S. regulatory commission for public communications. Its jurisdiction includes cable, radio and *satellite* communications. It is a party to international agreements on the frequency allocation of the *radio spectrum.*

feedback Signals or information that is taken from the output stage of a system and fed back to the input stage of a system.

ferrite core A ring-shaped piece of magnetic material. Depending on whether the ring is magnetized in a clockwise or counterclockwise direction, it will be used for storing binary 0 or binary 1. Rows of such cores are used as core store but may be replaced with semiconductor memory now.

ferro-resonance The resonance resulting when the iron core of an *inductor* that is part of an *LC circuit* is saturated, increasing the inductive reactance to the value of the capacitive reactance.

FET See *field effect transistor.*

FF See (1) *flip-flop;* (2) *form feed.*

fiber optics Fine threads of clear glass through which data is transmitted in the form of light waves generated by a laser.

fiber optics transmission system A data communications system that uses *optical fibers* instead of copper wire. The information is carried by modulating light. A transmission cable will consist of large bundles of these small lightweight nonconductive fibers.

fiber ribbon A ribbon made of textile or nylon, and treated with ink. Its print quality is acceptable, and it is inexpensive and lasts a long time. Compare *carbon ribbon.*

field A component of a record corresponding to one item of data. Field size or width is often used to indicate the extent of the item of data for input, storage and output operations. For example, a supplier record holds information fields for name, address and telephone number. The 'name' field size is 20 characters.

field effect transistor (FET) A semiconductor device that works by regulating the current as it flows through a narrow channel. They are smaller and cheaper than *bipolar transistors* and a greater density of *logic gates* on a *silicon chip* may be achieved with FETs.

field separator The character or group of characters that may be required in a *high level programming language* to separate individual sections (fields) of information for storage or printing, *e.g.* the comma (,) or semicolon (;) in *BASIC* print statements.

FIFO See *first in-first out.*

fifth generation computers Currently under development, they will use VLSI manufacturing techniques, and provide *parallel processing* with a number of processors working together. This will require new concepts in computer programming languages that concentrate on logic programming running on parallel machines. See also *first, second, third* and *fourth generation computers.*

file A collection of data, of any form, that is stored beyond the point in time when it is created and used. It may contain program instructions, or data that consists of numerical, textual or graphic information. In data processing, a file is a set of similar or related records that are treated in the same way.

file, archive See *archived file.*

file, back-up See *back-up.*

file, control totals See *check totals.*

file, copy The action of making a duplicate of an existing file for *back-up* or other purposes.

file, cycling See *ancestral file system.*

file, disk See *disk file.*

file, dump A copy of a file of computer-held data taken at a specific time for back-up, fault detection or general checking.

file, format The organization of information into collections of related data for computer processing.

file, indexed sequential See *indexed file.*

file, inverted See *inverted file.*

file, library A file held in an on-line disk *library* or magnetic tape library.

file, master See *master file.*

file, name A unique reference for each document/file so it can be filled, retrieved and edited.

file, output See *output file.*

file, random access See *random access* file.

file, reference See *reference file.*

file, rename The action of changing the name of a stored file.

file, save The action of storing a program file.

file, sequential See *sequential file.*

file, serial See *serial file.*

file, sort The action of *sorting* the records within a file according to some predetermined sequence.

file, transaction See *transaction file.*

file, update The action of entering a new record or changing the contents of a record in a file.

file, work See *work file.*

file access The action of storing or retrieving data from a file.

file descriptor Information that describes a file, giving such details as its name, generation number, date of last access, expiry date and structure of records. This information is usually held in a file *header block.*

file design factors Those factors affecting the design of a specific file structure, *e.g.* operational purpose, hardware, file size, output requirements, input requirements and file density.

file directory See *directory.*

file interrogation Accessing a file in order to retrieve information.

file label See *label.*

file maintenance Activities concerned with keeping data files accurate and complete. These include the provision of *back-up* copies, purging old or superseded records and the maintenance of a correct and efficient file structure.

file management The allocation of logical files to physical storage devices, and the selection of a suitable structure for each file.

file organization The technique used for organizing data records within a file. The choice of indexed sequential file, random access file or indexed file records will be influenced by the proposed media but generally is independent of the file access method.

file processing The set of activities by which data is stored in and retrieved from files.

file protection The protection of files and data in files, from inadvertent or unauthorized alteration and deletion. Some protection refers to the safe storage of file media, *e.g.* fireproof safes. Other physical constraints include *write-permit rings* or tabs that prevent files from being updated. File data record protection is usually managed by software controls such as *passwords* or *encryption* codes to enable users to access a file or part of a file.

file structure The structure of records and fields within a file.

file transfer Movement of a file from one computer to another in a network.

fill character A character used in transmission to fill an otherwise empty position and whose value is thus ignored.

financial modeling The use of a mathematical model that defines the relationships between different financial elements, *e.g.* stock item price, current level of stock, value of current stock holding.

financial planning packages Computer application software associated with financial planning, estimating and forecasting, usually requiring some form of *financial modeling.* See also *spreadsheet.*

firmware System software that is held in read only memory *(ROM).* It is not lost when the machine is switched off.

first generation computers Computers developed between 1940 and 1952, constructed with vacuum tubes providing internal operating speeds of the order of milliseconds, using punch cards and paper tape as input media, predominantly programmed in machine code and symbolic languages. The main disadvantages were the large size, the amount of generated heat and hence the need for air conditioning, the unreliability and constant maintenance to provide only simple batch processing facilities. See also *second, third, fourth* and *fifth generation computers.*

first in-first out (FIFO) Another name for a *queue.*

fixed-count check A check to determine whether a bit pattern has a required number of 1 bits.

fixed disk A disk that cannot be removed from the *disk drive, e.g.* Winchester disk. Compare *exchangeable disk, hard disk.*

fixed head disk drive A *disk drive* that has a *read/write* head positioned over every disk track. Thus the head does not move relative to the center of the disk. Instead the disk revolves until a head is over the required position for reading or writing data.

fixed-instruction computer A computer in which the sequence of *instruction* sets is fixed by the manufacturer.

fixed length record A record in which the number of bits or characters of information has been predetermined.

fixed point notation A representation of real numbers, expressed by a set of digits with the decimal point in its correct position, *e.g.* 133.479. During operations in the computer, the position of the decimal point is generally maintained by the program. Compare *floating point notation.*

fixed word length computer A computer in which data is constrained to lie within words that are all of the same length. Compare *variable word length computer.*

flag A variable whose value indicates the state of a condition and is used for conditional branching within program code, *e.g.* whether a file has been sorted, whether an *interrupt* has been sensed.

flag lines Inputs to a microprocessor controlled by *I/O* devices and tested by *branch* instructions.

flat bed plotter A *plotter* that holds the paper on a flat surface. The movable bars, mounted parallel to the side and over the paper, can move a pen accurately to any x or y coordinate.

flexible machining system (FMS) *Numerically controlled* machines that carry out a number of operations on different work pieces without routine human intervention.

flexible manufacturing system (FMS) A more recent use of *flexible machining system* applied to all types of manufacturing and production equipment, not restricted to metal cutting activities.

flip-flop (FF) A basic electronic circuit that remains in one of two possible states until it receives a signal. It then switches over to the other state and waits for the next signal before switching back. It is the common name for a *bistable multivibrator.*

flip screen A useful facility for instantly interrupting current work in order to perform a rush job. Pressing a key immediately transfers current work on the screen to a buffer memory and clears the screen for new work. Another touch of the key restores the original text to the screen.

floating point notation A representation of numbers expressed as a fractional value (*mantissa*) followed by an integer *exponent* of the base, *e.g.* 12.34 would have a mantissa of .1234 and an exponent of 2. Compare *fixed point notation.*

floating point numbers See *floating point notation.*

floppy disk A lightweight flexible magnetic disk that behaves as if it were rigid when rotated at high speed.

floppy disk controller The hardware or circuit board used to interface the floppy-disk drive with the microcomputer bus.

floppy disk drive A peripheral storage device into which a floppy disk may be inserted and from which data may be read or written to.

flowchart A simple graphical representation of the structure of a program. It usually consists of a set of boxes of various meaningful shapes to depict the different action or decision processes. These are interconnected with lines indicating the flow of control.

flowchart symbols The *flowchart* symbols defined by the American Society of Mechanical Engineers (ASME).

flush left A format for copy that maintains an even left margin.

flush right A format for copy that maintains an even right margin.

FM Frequency modulation. See *modulation.*

FMS See (1) *flexible machining system;* (2) *flexible manufacturing system.*

folding machine A machine that automatically folds documents and is especially useful for those that are mailed without an outer cover.

font A set of characters of a particular style and type used for printing.

footer Text which appears at the foot of each page of a document.

footing A short piece of text or other information, such as date and reference, that appears at the bottom of every page of a document.

footnote A piece of text that appears at the bottom of a page. It is referenced by a number and elaborates on material contained within the main text.

forced page break The characters or symbols inserted in word processing text that force a new page when the document is displayed or printed.

foreground processing Processing that supports interaction in a system when both interactive and batch processing facilities are available. See also *background processing.*

foreground program In a multiprogramming environment, a program that has a high priority and takes precedence over other programs of the EDP system.

form A page of printer media. See also *fanfold paper, continuous form paper, multipart stationery.*

form feed (FF) A signal sent to the printer to move the paper up to a predefined point at the beginning of the next sheet. Also called paper throw or *paper slew.*

form handling equipment The range of equipment for handling computer output, *i.e. collator, burster,* etc.

form letter A letter prepared for sending to many people. Often, provision is made for inserting information that varies from one person to another, such as name, address and salutation.

form overlay As an alternative to *preprinted stationery,* a form overlay is stored and printed out with the variable data.

form stop A sensor on a printer that generates a signal to indicate that there is insufficient paper to allow printing to continue.

format (1) The defined structure of the pattern of information that is recorded on *magnetic media,* displayed on a *VDU* or printed on a page; (2) to put data into a predetermined structure or divide a storage medium such as a disk into *sectors* ready to receive data.

format control code A *character* or sequence of characters used to adjust the placement of copy on a video screen or a printed page.

format line (ruler line) A line displayed on a VDT screen to show information about the appearance of the document being worked on.

formatted disk A disk which has been prepared to accept and store files.

forms design The format used for outputting computer data on paper. Aspects that affect design include: heading, all relevant information, any instructions, choice of wording, layout, printer specification and output materials.

forms tractor A device which uses revolving *sprockets* to pull *continuous form paper* through the *printer.*

FORTH A programming language that is popular with *microcomputer* users. A vital feature is the ability to associate a symbol (word) with any program string. Such user-defined words can be used in expressions on equal terms with the system words.

FORTRAN A programming language developed around 1956, primarily for scientific computing applications. The original version was issued by IBM and subsequently FORTRAN II and FORTRAN IV were developed. This latter was standardized by *ANSI* and known as FORTRAN 66. FORTRAN 77 is now in standard use and FORTRAN 88 is expected during the 1980s.

four-bit system A basic microcomputer logic *code* capable of handling information in groups of 4 *bits* or pulses.

fourth generation computers Computers developed from 1971 to the end of the 1980s, constructed with *VLSI* circuits providing internal operating speeds of the order of picoseconds, using magnetic tape, OCR, MICR, magnetic cards and bar codes as input media, predominantly programmed in high level languages. See also *first, second, third* and *fifth generation computers.*

frame A single packet of information such as a section of magentic tape comprising a single bit in each track, a single message on a data link.

free space media Free space is utilized for transmission between aerials or radiation sources and sensors, *e.g. communication satellites* use free space media. See also *bounded media.*

freedom of information A phrase that may be used in various contexts: (1) lack of censorship; (2) deregulation of the communications media, the removal of restrictions on the use of *broadcasting* frequencies and communication cables; (3) fair use of *copyright* material; (4) rights of an individual to study computer based records; (5) transfer of high technology information to third world countries.

frequency The number of complete cycles of a periodically variable quantity, such as a pulse or wave, that occurs in unit time. For a.c. circuits, it designates the number of times that polarity alternates from positive to negative and back again. It is measured in Hertz, *e.g.* 60 cycles per second is 60Hz.

frequency modulation (FM) See *modulation.*

frequency variation A deviation from the normal *frequency.* Frequency variations are usually caused by large load changes in the power system. The magnitude of the variation depends on the magnitude of the load change. Duration depends on how fast the system recovers from the change.

friction feed A mechanism for advancing paper in a printer by gripping it between rollers. Compare *tractor feed.*

front end processor An I/O processor that is used to organize and/or process input data. The term is sometimes used to refer to a communications processor that coordinates all transmission between the main computer and its terminals. See also *back end processor.*

full duplex A form of serial data transmission in which two data *links* are running side by side, one in each direction.

full size display A *VDU* display capable of showing a full page of text. Most screens only display part of a page.

full formed character Pertaining to *printers* that produce an individual character display with a single action.

function (1) A *character* or *string* that defines a relation between some combination of *constants* and *variables*, *e.g.* in 2 op 3 = 6, op is the function 'times.' (2) A Pascal subprogram that operates on an arbitrary number of *arguments* to return a single result.

function character A *character* of a data-representation code that has special meaning when read by a particular type of device.

function keys Keys beyond the normal *QWERTY* keyboard layout. These keys provide special facilities for communicating with the computer. In some cases they have predefined functions for controlling text generation or message transmission and in other cases they may be programmed to perform special functions under the control of software.

function specification Documentation that states the effects that a software module is required to achieve. It does not prescribe how different features and functions will be achieved.

functional unit Any major component of a computing system, *e.g.* main memory, CPU, peripheral device.

fuzzy theory A branch of logic designed specifically for representing knowledge and human reasoning in such a way that it is amenable to processing by computer, *e.g.*

degrees of uncertainty are allowed compared to the normal two state conditions of true or false, right or wrong. Fuzzy theory is applicable to *expert systems, knowledge engineering* and *artificial intelligence.*

G

G See *giga-*.

game paddle A general name for a hand held control device used for computer games.

game theory A mathematical theory of decision making by participants with conflicting interests in a competitive situation.

Gantt chart See *bar chart.*

garbage Unwanted or unexpected data.

garbage collection (1) The collection of dead *records* from a file. (2) The rearrangement of *storage* with the deletion of unwanted items.

Garbage in, garbage out (GIGO) An anacronym signifying that a system working on incorrect data produces incorrect results.

gate An electronic switch or circuit which passes or stops the flow of current, signals or pulses.

gateway A link between networks.

general purpose computer A computer that can be used for any function for which it can be conveniently programmed.

generate To use a *program generator* to construct a *machine-language* program from a set of specifications.

generations of computers An informal system of classifying computer systems, primarily according to the electronic technology used for their manufacture. See also *first, second, third, fourth* and *fifth generation computers.*

generator See *program generator.*

germanium A chemical element used for making semiconductor devices in the 1950s, now largely replaced by *silicon.*

ghost cursor A secondary pointer available on some word processing systems that appears when doing a secondary task during input or editing; the main cursor fades when the ghost is on the screen.

giga- (G) A prefix to a unit indicating a multiple of one thousand million, *e.g.* 1×10^9 bytes is a gigabyte.

GIGO See *garbage in, garbage out.*

GINO A package of *FORTRAN subroutines* for computer *graphics.*

glare Strong, fierce reflected light that is unwanted and unpleasant.

global network An intercontinental communications network.

global search and replace The ability to automatically change the same word or phrase throughout a piece of text or program. It is a useful feature of *editors* and word processing software.

global variable A *variable* that is accessible from all parts of a program. See also *local variable.*

glossary functions The storage of commonly used phrases, such as signature blocks. Each phrase is identified by a code and can be inserted anywhere in a document.

golf ball printer A printer that uses a spherical print head. The head is easily removable, enabling many different *character sets* to be inserted.

graceful degradation The ability of a system to keep running even if some parts fail.

grandfather file See *ancestral file system.*

graph plotter See *x-y plotter.*

graphics A mode of computer processing and output in which a significant part of the output information is in pictorial form. The information may range from a simple *histogram* or other plot of information to a complex map or engineering design annotated with *alphanumerics* and displayed in color. The output may be via a visual display terminal or as a permanent record via a printer, *plotter* or *x-y recorder.* Suitable input devices include *graphics tablets* and *light pens.*

graphics tablet An input device where the movement of a pen over a sensitive pad is translated into *digital signals* giving the pen's position.

graphics VDU A *VDU* with special facilities to display graphs, charts and diagrams using *high resolution graphics.*

grid chart A two dimensional table used to express relationships between two types of *entities.*

guard A mechanism to terminate *program execution* upon access to data at a specified memory location. Used in *debugging.*

guillotine equipment Office equipment to trim sheets of paper prior to distribution. It may be part of complex equipment attached to a computer for bursting, decollating and guillotining computer output.

H

hacker A programmer who obsessively tinkers with computer systems, producing more or less useful additional features that tend to be badly documented and may have unfortunate side effects. Used more recently to imply deliberate sabotage or interference with systems which the programmer should not be accessing.

half duplex operation A transmission system that allows data to be transmitted in both directions but only in one direction at any one time. Compare *full duplex* and *simplex operation.*

handheld terminal A variation on the full *keyboard* device that is smaller, with a few keys oriented to the data entry application, *e.g.* an order entry or stock recording terminal.

hands off See *hands on.*

hands on A mode of operation of a system in which an *operator* is in control. The operator literally has hands on a *keyboard* and other switches to control the processing. When no operator intervention is required, the mode of operation can be described as *hands off.*

handshaking The exchange of predetermined signals to establish communication between two devices and permit data to be transferred across an *interface.*

hang-up A state in which a program has come to an unexpected halt, *e.g.* because it is trying to send output to a device which is not switched on. In the case of *time* sharing systems, a hang-up occurs when a *remote terminal* connection is broken.

hard copy A printed or otherwise permanent copy of data from a processing system.

hard disk A rigid magnetic disk. It normally allows a higher recording density than a *floppy disk,* thus providing more storage for the same physical dimensions. On a PC, a hard disk is a *fixed disk.*

hard error A *permanent error* within the data or media. Compare *transient error.*

hard hyphen A *required hyphen* keyed by the operator.

hard return A return entered manually by the operator; *e.g.* at the end of a paragraph.

hard sectored disk The start of each *sector* on the disk is related to a sector signal generated by the *disk drive* and is positively related to the position of the disk. This technique permits higher packing of sectors as intersector gaps are not necessary to accommodate speed variations. See also *soft sectored disk.*

hardware The physical portion of a computer system, including the electrical/electronic components (devices and circuits), electromechanical components (disk drive, printer, etc.) and mechanical components (cabinets).

hardware reliability A statement of the ability of hardware to perform its function for a specific period of time. It is often expressed as *mean time between failures.*

hardware security The use of hardware security measures such as locks, keys or access cards which are required before the equipment will function.

hardwired Refers to those circuits that are permanently interconnected to perform a specific function, as distinct from circuits addressed by software and capable of a variety of functions.

hardwired terminal Those terminals that are physically close to the computer system and are connected by a direct cable. See also *remote terminal.*

harmonic The sinusoidal component of an *a.c. voltage* that is a multiple of the fundamental waveform *frequency.*

harmonic distortion The presence of *harmonics* that change an *a.c. voltage* waveform from sinusoidal to complex.

Harvard Mark 1 The name given at Harvard University to the Automatic Sequence Controlled Calculator (ASCC) which follows instructions from a paper tape. It became operational in 1944 and was used by the U.S. Navy for ballistics and ship design.

hash function A function used for *hashing.*

hash totals A number produced by adding together (or otherwise combining) corresponding fields over all records in a file. The number may have no external meaning; but when the file is subsequently used, the hash totals may be checked and differences will occur when records have been changed.

hashing A technique for generating numbers which are used to assist in organizing *tables* to permit rapid searching or *table lookup.* It is particularly useful for tables where items are added in an unpredictable way, *e.g.* adding records to file structures.

HDLC See *high level data link control.*

head The mechanism that reads information from, or writes information to, the secondary *storage media.*

head crash The dramatic and often expensive descent of a *read/write head* onto the surface of a disk, caused by mechanical malfunction.

head switching The activation of the *read/write head* that is to read/write data by a *direct access storage device.*

header Some coded information that precedes a more general collection of data when it is being stored. The header provides details about the data structure to enable the information to be updated and/or retrieved. See also *heading* for the text processing use of header.

header block A block of information placed at the beginning of a *telex* message that holds the appropriate details about the message recipient. See also *header* and *heading.*

header sheets Instruction sheets which are read by an *optical character reader* (OCR). The header sheets tell the reader what typeface, line spacing, and other format to look for on the documents that follow.

heading A short piece of text or other information such as a title that appears on the top of every page in a document.

heapsort A method of sorting developed by Williams and Floyd in 1964 and employing the ideas of *tree selection sort.* It is more efficient for larger numbers of records but on average is inferior to *quicksort.*

Hertz (Hz) The unit of a.c. current *frequency* measurement.

heuristic program A program so written that each time it solves a problem, it stores the result for subsequent use. For example, traffic control systems respond to pressure pads indicating traffic flow. Having adjusted a light sequence, the system can monitor the resultant traffic movement or buildup of lines and use the information to adjust how it responds to the next change in traffic conditions.

.HEX In either CP/M or MP/M, the *extension* for a file containing an executable program in *hex-intel format.* The LOAD program can be used to convert it to a .COM file.

hex Short for hexadecimal. See also *hexadecimal notation.*

hex pad A *keypad* with 16 keys corresponding to the *hexadecimal notation.*

hexadecimal notation A number system that uses a base of 16 and the digits 0,1,2,3,4,5,6,7,8,9,A,B,C,D,E,F.

hex-intel format A standard format for storing binary information on paper tape, disk or magnetic tape.

HF See *high frequency.*

HFFC See *horizontal form flowchart symbols.*

hidden line algorithm An *algorithm* used in graph plotting, etc., to determine which lines should not be visible when a three dimensional surface is plotted.

hierarchical codes Sometimes called decimal codes, these codes use a classification system whereby a decimal point is inserted to subdivide the code into several significant stages. The most obvious example is the Universal Decimal Code (UDC) used in book classification:

3	Social Sciences
37	Education
372	Elementary
372.2	Kindergarten

hierarchical communication system An interconnection structure composed of several levels or groupings, each higher level covering a wider or more general area of operation than the next lower level.

hierarchical data base A *data base management system* in which there is a data hierarchy whereby each record is 'owned' by another record (its owner), and each member record type may be owned by only one record type. Compare with *network data base system.*

high frequency (HF) A band of *radio frequencies* between 3MHz and 30MHz, usually used for shortwave radio transmissions, ship radio telephone, etc.

high level data link control (HDLC) A data link control protocol developed by *ISO* in response to IBM's *SDLC* protocol.

high level programming language A type of *programming language* in which the instructions reflect the requirements of the *programmer* rather than the facilities and method of operation provided by the hardware. A high level language is translated into *machine code* by a *compiler.*

high resolution graphics The quality of the graphical information that can be shown on a visual display will be termed high resolution if the numbers of *pixels* ensure that circles and diagonal lines do not appear as a series of small stepped lines. See also *resolution.*

highlighting A facility which identifies and emphasizes certain text on the *screen* by brightening either the *characters* or the background.

high-order Pertaining to the digits that have the most significance in a numeral.

histogram A chart showing the relative frequencies with which a measurable quantity takes values in a set of contiguous intervals. The chart consists of rectangles whose areas are proportional to the relative frequencies and whose widths are proportional to the class intervals.

HMI Human-machine interaction or interface. See *man-machine interface.*

holdup The length of time a power supply's output voltage remains within specification following the loss of input power.

Hollerith code A code widely used for representing data on 80-column *punched cards.*

hologram A photographic system that uses *laser* light to create a three dimensional image.

holographic memory A storage device that records binary information in the form of holograms, which are produced (as interference patterns) on photographic or photochromic media by means of laser beams, and are read by means of low power laser beams.

home The name given to the top left hand side of the screen, especially used with *cursor* control for word processing.

home computer system A term used to describe any small *microcomputer* system, commonly bought for use in the home for playing games or learning about computers and programming.

hopper A device that holds *punched cards* ready for feeding to a *card punch* or *card reader.*

horizontal form flowchart symbols (HFFC) Flowchart symbols used in systems procedures to represent activities and events symbolically.

host computer A computer that is attached to a network and provides services other than simply acting as a *store and forward* processor or a communication switching station.

hot zone Also called soft zone, this is an area in a line of text to the left of the right hand *margin* in a word processed document. The zone is adjustable and any word which starts in the hot zone but will not fit completely is detected by the software and a hyphen can be inserted.

housekeeping Actions performed within a program or system, either automatically or by *operator* control, to maintain order or security, *e.g.* sequences to maintain *back-up* copies of files and reorganize internal memory use to optimize processing.

human factors engineering The study of how people and technology can work in harmony; basically the same as *ergonomics.*

human-machine interaction or interface (HMI) See *man-machine interface.*

hybrid computer A computer system consisting of an analog and a digital computer. The *digital computer* usually serves as the controller and provides logical operations; the *analog computer* normally serves as a solver of differential equations.

hyphen A character in the form of a dash which indicates that the word in a piece of text is not yet complete. Some words require a hyphen whenever they are used, *e.g.* user-friendly. See also *hyphenation, rehyphenation, discretionary hyphen* and *required hyphen.*

hyphenation The division of a word of text into two parts if the total word is too long for the available space at the end of a printed line. The first part of the word is ended with a *hyphen.*

Hz See *Hertz.*

I

IAL See *international algorithmic language.*

IAR See *instruction address register.*

IAS See *immediate access store.*

IBG See *interblock gap.*

IC See *integrated circuit.*

icon A screen symbol representing a particular function, *e.g.* a symbol shaped like a file folder to represent the filing function.

IDA See *integrated digital access.*

identifier A string of characters used to identify some element of a program. The kind of element will depend on the programming language; it may be a *variable,* a *procedure,* a *statement,* a *label,* a higher level unit or the program itself.

IDP Integrated data processing. Data processing in which data acquisition and other stages of data processing are coordinated into one system.

IEEE Institute of Electrical and Electronic Engineers.

IFIP See *International Federation for Information Processing.*

IH See *interrupt handler.*

IIL See *integrated injection logic.*

ikon See *icon.*

ILF See *infralow frequency.*

image processing See *picture processing.*

immediate access store (IAS) A memory device in which the *access time* for any location is independent of the previous access. The time is usually of the same order as the cycle time of the processor and such devices are normally only used for main memory.

immediate addressing The situation where the address field itself is used to hold the data needed for the operation. See also *indirect addressing.*

immediate mode This is the use, for immediate execution, of a program language statement outside the program.

impact printer A term applied to any printer where the standard typewriter action of 'character pressing on paper through inked ribbon' is used, *e.g. chain printer, daisy wheel printer.* See also *nonimpact printer.*

impedance The ratio of the *r.m.s.* value of the *voltage* applied to an electric circuit, to the *current* flowing in the circuit.

incremental plotter A device that can draw graphs and other line images when fed with digital data. The plotter forms the image by moving a pen or the paper or both in a succession of increments. The increments are typically 200 per inch for *drum plotters* and can be 500 per inch for *flatbed plotters.* Compare with *x-y plotter.*

indentation White space a specified number of positions from either the right or left margin of a body of text.

index Generally, the mechanism, computer orientated or manual, in which a data value is presented to an ordered list that contains a location at which further searching for the data item should be continued.

index register A register that can be specified by instructions that use *indexed addressing.* An index register is usually controlled by one or more instructions with the ability to increment or decrement the register by a fixed amount.

index word A *storage location* containing a quantity that may be added to or subtracted from an address prior to or during *execution* of an instruction.

indexed addressing The situation where the direct or indirect address is further modified by the addition of a number held in a special purpose register, called an index register.

indexed file A file whose organization uses an *index.* The index may be separated from the file as in the case of a book, or located within the file, as in the case of a telephone directory. If the file is sequential, an index may be based upon the data item on which the file is ordered. In this case it is usually called a primary index and the file is called an *indexed sequential file.* Alternatively, the index may be upon a data item that is not the one used for ordering and in that case it is known as a secondary index.

indexed sequential file See *indexed file.*

indexing See *indexed addressing.*

indirect addressing A method of addressing where the address in one program instruction refers to another location that contains another address. The technique is used by programmers to access a series of addresses with just one instruction whose address is increased by one each time it is carried out.

indirect phase A predetermined state of microcomputer logic which causes the microprocessor to interpret as an *address* information read out of memory during a memory cycle.

inductance A measure of *induction.* One henry is the inductance of a circuit in which a rate of change of current of 1 ampere per second gives rise to an induced e.m.f. of 1 volt.

induction A term associated with the density of a magnetic or electric field created by the changing flow of an electrical current.

inductor A *conductor,* usually coiled, that tends to oppose any change in the flow of *current* through itself.

industrial robot See *robot.*

infix A form of algebraic notation in which *operators* are placed between the *operands, e.g.* A + B, X AND Y. Infix notation requires the use of brackets to specify the order of evaluation.

informatics The study of human aspects of information, *i.e.* quality, value, utilization, etc.

information Collections of symbols, which subsequently form patterns that carry meaning to the observer. The patterns that constitute information may be created in a diversity of forms including: light, sound or radio waves; electric current or voltage; magnetic fields; marks on paper.

information center The center in an organization whose responsibilities include providing advice on office automation services, developments in new technology and information processing.

information line Part of the permanent display that provides information processing operatives with information about the status of the equipment. It can include names of files, status of processing, available functions, run time, etc., for general applications and may include document titles, page numbers and character positions for word processing.

information processing The organization, manipulation and distribution of information.

information processor A computer that can process both data and text.

information provider (IP) The individuals or organizations with contracts to provide information pages for broadcast information services.

information retrieval The activity of retrieving stored information. The term is usually associated with computer information storage systems but it can equally apply to the manual retrieval of information.

information storage The activity of recording information for subsequent use, usually on *backing store, e.g.* magnetic disk or tape.

information storage and retrieval (ISR) This refers not only to the activities of *information storage* and *information retrieval* but to the many types of techniques involved in handling these processes.

information system A computer based service that provides information in response to specific requests from users. It may be operated by an organization for their own benefit or offered to the public on a subscription basis.

information technology (IT) Incorporates the technologies involved with computing, word processing, telecommunications, consumer electronics and *broadcasting.* Applications are business, industrial, commercial, administrative, educational, medical, scientific, professional and domestic.

information theory The study of information by mathematical methods. For example, information theory is used to estimate the limits of accurate information that may be carried by some physical medium such as magnetic tape. It also includes how messages should be represented so that when they are transmitted via a given carrier the decoded message will contain a minimum of errors.

infralow frequency (ILF) A band of radio frequencies between 300Hz and 3KHz, usually used for voice transmission.

in-house Taking place within the organization, rather than outside.

initial program load (IPL) The first action of loading the *operating system* software into a machine after the power is switched on.

initialization The act of assigning initial values to *variables* before the start of a computation.

ink jet printer A printer that produces characters when a fine jet of quick drying ink is fired at the paper. The ink droplets become charged as they are fired through the jet and are bent into shape by a varying electric field. Speeds as high as 200 characters per second can be achieved.

inline processing A technique in which data is accepted for processing as it is generated without preliminary sorting or editing and without being collected in batches.

input device Any device that transfers data, programs or signals into a processor system. Such devices provide a *man-machine interface, e.g. keyboard, data tablet,* *light pen, magnetic strip reader, bar code reader* and *OCR* equipment.

input/output (I/O) A prefix applied to the different activities associated with the transfer of information into or out of the central processing unit in a computer system, *e.g.* I/O buffers, I/O devices, I/O port, etc.

input/output buffer See *buffer.*

input/output bus A *bus* that connects input and output channels/devices.

input/output channel A *channel* used for input or output communications.

input/output device A device for handling *I/O.*

input/output file A file used for input or output.

input/output instruction An *instruction* concerned with input or output processes.

input/output port A *port* used for input or output processes.

inrush current The peak instantaneous input *current* drawn by the power supply at turn-on.

insert To add new items to an existing set of items, *e.g.* adding characters, lines or other portions of text to existing text in word processing applications or adding a record to an existing set of records in a file.

instruction The description of an operation that is to be performed by a computer.

instruction address register (IAR) This *register* stores in turn the *addresses* of the instructions that the computer has to carry out.

instruction code The arrangement of *bits* which tells the microcomputer to execute a particular *instruction.*

instruction counter An internal computer component that indicates the location of the next *instruction* to be executed.

instruction register See *control unit.*

insulator A material that has a very high *resistance* to electric *current* so that the current flow through it is negligible.

integer Any positive, negative or zero whole number.

integrate To combine parts into one unit.

integrated circuit (IC) A solid state circuit in which all the components are formed upon a single piece of semiconductor material. See *large scale integration, medium scale integration, reticle, small scale integration,* and *very large scale integration.*

integrated data processing (IDP) Data processing using facilities to coordinate and optimize the use and manipulation of data. This is usually achieved with data base systems.

integrated digital access (IDA) Digital transmission networks linked to a subscriber's premises, enabling a user to make two phone calls and access a data base or send a page through a facsimile receiver simultaneously.

integrated injection logic (IIL) A semiconductor device technology for a logic family, fabricated using *bipolar* techniques. This permits a higher packing density of individual devices in a single chip and a reduction in the complexity of chip fabrication.

integrated office See *electronic office.*

integrated office automation *Electronic office* components that have been combined to provide linked, coherent information technology facilities.

integrated software A combination of two or more software *applications* on one disk.

integrated voice/data terminal A terminal designed for document input, text editing, voice communications and data communications.

intelligent copier Document copying equipment with *microprocessor* circuitry that provides a range of programmable facilities.

intelligent front end See *front end processor.*

intelligent terminal A terminal device with some independent processing capability. This enables information to be transferred to and from a larger processing system or alternatively processing may be carried out without further access to the main system. Compare *dumb terminal.*

INTELSAT See *International Telecommunications Satellite Organization.*

interactive cable TV A *cable television* system capable of both sending and receiving back information from subscribers.

interactive processing A mode of computer operation where the currently active program is designed to stop at one or more points to enable the user to enter information that could affect that program's subsequent course of action.

interactive system A system where there is a response to user instructions as they are entered. This mode of working is sometimes referred to as *conversational mode* and an interactive system for multiple users will achieve the effect by *time sharing.* See also *multiaccess system.*

interactive terminal A terminal capable of both sending and receiving data as required by an *interactive system.*

interactive video Laser disk video equipment is connected to a microcomputer and a combination of presentation and user interaction is controlled via suitable software.

interblock gap (IBG) The spacing between *blocks* of information on a specific medium, *e.g.* magnetic tape IBG.

intercharacter spacing The process of adding spaces between words in order to justify text.

interface A common boundary between two systems, devices or programs. An interface can consist of signal connections and circuitry that is transparent to a system user or the interface can be a common language or set of commands that link the user to a system, *i.e.* user interface.

interleaving A similiar process to *overlay* whereby segments from different jobs are brought from *backing store* for processing in a *multiprogramming system.*

intermediate document These documents are usually used for collecting data from service documents and providing summaries from which reports can be written.

internal data transfer The movement of data from one location in main storage to another.

internal telephone systems There are three main systems: *PAX, PMBX* and *PABX.*

international algorithmic language (IAL) The original name for the language later called *ALGOL 58.*

international direct dialing (IDD) The facility that enables telephone subscribers to dial direct to many places overseas.

International Federation for Information Processing (IFIP) An organization that came into official existence during 1960 as the International Federation of Information Processing Societies. It aims to 'promote information science and technology, advance international cooperation in the field of information processing, stimulate research, development and application of information processing, further dissemination and exchange of information in information processing, and encourage education in information processing.' It has members in more than 41 countries.

International Standards Organization (ISO) The body by which international standards are established for everything from data processing equipment to sizes of engineering components. It was founded in 1946 and its members comprise national standards bodies in over 70 countries.

International Telecommunications Satellite Organization (ITSO) Sometimes abbreviated to Intelsat, this 109-nation organization operates 14 communication satellites in the current Intelsat V series.

International Telecommunications Union (ITU) An agency of the United Nations.

internet protocol (IP) The *DARPA protocol* that links defense research centers in the U.S.A. and Europe using underlying networks such as *ARPANET, satellite networks* and many different *local area networks.*

interpreter A *program* that accepts as input a series of *high-level* commands and executes them as it goes, rather than saving them as machine instructions.

interpreting keyboard Data preparation equipment that has the facility to prepare punch cards and interpret them by printing the data across the top of the card.

interrecord gap (IRG) An interval of space or time left between recording portions of data or records to prevent errors.

interrogation See *file interrogation.*

interrupt A signal, generated by a source such as an input or output device, which causes a break in the execution of the current routine. Control passes to another routine in such a way that afterwards the original routine may be resumed.

interrupt handler (IH) A section of code to which control is transferred when a processor is interrupted.

in-use light A red light on a *disk drive* which lights up when the system is performing read or write operations on the disk in the drive.

inversion operator See *NOT function.*

inverted file A file provided with a secondary index on one or more of its data items (fields). In the case where indexes exist for all the data items of a record, the file is said to be fully inverted. For example, in an uninverted file, there is a succession of records each with a number of data items or fields. If the number of occurrences of a particular field value was required, each record would need to be read and examined for a field match.

inverter a.c.-d.c. A device that changes *alternating current* to *direct current* or vice versa.

invocation The activation of a *subprogram* by referring to its name and supplying it with an appropriate list of *arguments* on which to operate.

I/O See *input/output.*

I/O controller The unit that enables the *CPU* to transfer data to or from a *peripheral* device.

IP See *internet protocol.*

IPL See *initial program load.*

ISBN International Standard Book Number.

ISO See *International Standards Organization.*

isolation transformer A *transformer* of multiple windings with primary and secondary windings physically separated. It is designed to provide magnetic coupling (flux coupling) between one or more pairs of isolated circuits, without introducing significant coupling of any other kind between them.

ISR See *information storage and retrieval.*

IT See *information technology.*

iteration A method of obtaining a result by repeatedly performing the same sequence of steps until a specified condition is satisfied.

I-time Instruction time. The time required to move an *instruction* from *main storage* to the *address* and *operation code* registers.

ITSO See *International Telecommunications Satellite Organization* (Intelsat).

ITU See *International Telecommunications Union.*

IVI Iinteractive video instruction. A combination of computers and *video disk* players that enables programs to incorporate prerecorded *graphics.*

J

jack plug A type of plug that offers quick and easy connection in that its single pin is pushed into a socket as far as it will go.

JCL See *job control language.*

job control file A file containing job control language instructions for processing.

job control language (JCL) A language used to write the sequence of commands that will control the running of a job. In a JCL the objects manipulated are such items as complete programs, input and output channels for the programs and sequences of processing with alternative actions when system/program errors are detected.

job control program An operating-system program that reads job control statements describing work to be performed by the computer.

job mix The set of jobs being executed within a multiprogramming system at any one time. See also *scheduler.*

job monitoring The control of the jobs running within a system. The term is almost synonymous with *job scheduling.*

job number A number allocated by the operating system in order to differentiate between users or jobs.

job oriented language Any language that enables a programmer to easily express the problem or processing required as compared to languages that are designed to fit a machine, *i.e. machine oriented languages.*

job queue A sequence of jobs awaiting processing.

job scheduling Selecting jobs for execution. See also *scheduler.*

job step A single identifiable execution of a program on its data within a job. Each job step produces an error indication if the process is not successful, ensuring that subsequent job steps can be bypassed within the JCL if necessary.

job stream See *job queue.*

Josephson memory A form of memory device that uses *Josephenson (junction) technology.*

Josephson (junction) technology A technology based on superconductivity and electron tunneling between metals. These effects occur at very low temperatures, usually obtained by immersing the whole system in liquid helium. *Logic circuits* and *nonvolatile memories* can be made which have the potential for ultrafast switching speeds and very low power dissipation.

journal See *transaction file.*

joystick An input device for a microcomputer or electronic game. It is a convenient form of *analog-digital converter* where input is the movement of a control lever in two dimensions, *e.g.* simulating the direction controls required for flying a plane.

jump vector A jump or *branch* instruction that transfers control to a specific *subroutine* or function.

junction transistor Sometimes called the *bipolar transistor* or just 'transistor,' this semiconductor device works by regulating the current across a junction or boundary between p-type and n-type materials. These transistors are faster acting than the *field effect transistor.*

justification The process of inserting tiny spaces between letters in a word, or between words themselves, to make the last letter of a line appear at the right *margin.* Justified text looks like a column. See also *unjustified text* and *ragged text.*

justified margins Right and left *margins* flush, or straight, as opposed to ragged.

justify left To set text to print with an even left *margin.*

justify right To set text to print with an even right *margin.*

K

k See *kilo-*.

Kansas City standard A cassette-tape protocol designed in the early days of microcomputers for data transferral.

Karnaugh map A tabulator arrangement for simplifying logical functions.

key (1) A switch on a keyboard labeled with a character. (2) A value used to identify a member of a set. Usually the members of a set are records in which one of the fields holds the key. (3) A value used to establish authority to access particular information. (4) A value used as a basis for data encryption.

key field The record field holding the unique information that is used to identify any specific record.

key punch A device having a keyboard, a hopper for supplying cards and a stacker for taking the cards when they have been punched. Some key punches only punch holes in the cards while others interpret the characters by printing a corresponding row of symbols on the top of the card.

key to disk A device that allows data from a keyboard to be entered directly onto a disk storage medium.

key to tape A device that allows data from a keyboard to be entered directly onto a magnetic tape storage medium.

keyboard A collection of switches, keys, buttons or

marked areas on a board that are used to communicate with a processing device or system. The most frequently used key layout follows the standard *QWERTY* typewriter keyboard. The operation of a key is detected and turned into a signal to punch a hole in a card or paper tape, print a symbol or send a character to a processor.

keyboarding The keying in of text (numbers, letters and symbols) in order to interact with a computer application package such as word processing.

keypad An input device used for specialized data entry—usually with 10 digits and some control keys for numeric data.

keystrip A strip of paper that fits above the programmable *function keys* on a computer keyboard. It describes the function of each key. Compare *template.*

keystroke One press of a single key on the keyboard.

keyword A symbol in a *programming language* that has a specially defined meaning for a *compiler* or *interpreter.* They are sometimes referred to as reserved words.

keyword search When computer information is searched by specifying the words that will identify the items required.

kilo- (K or k) A prefix to a unit indicating a multiple of 1000, *e.g.* 1×10^3. In computing applications K is often used to denote a multiple of 1024, *i.e.* 2^{10}. Typical examples are 64K bytes or 64 kilobytes or 65,536 characters of storage and 96 kilobaud for 96,000 bits per second for data transmission.

kilobyte One thousand bytes.

kilo volt-ampere output rating (kVA) This designates the output that a unit can deliver continuously without exceeding its component ratings (1kVA = 1000VA).

Kimball tag A small punched card attached to merchandise that is ultimately detached when goods are sold, to provide machine readable sales data. Variations now hold information on magnetic strips.

kips Thousands (K) of instructions per second. A unit for indicating the processing capacity of a computer.

knowledge based system See *expert system.*

knowledge engineering The methodology for building *expert systems.*

L

label A statement label is a numeric or alphabetic identifier associated with a line or statement in a program and used in other parts of the program to refer to that statement.

label field The field associated with the label in an *assembly language* instruction.

lagging load An inductive type load.

LAN See *local area network.*

language See *programming language.*

language translation Using computer processing to translate *natural languages*, *e.g.* Japanese to English. Most systems are only 80 to 85 percent efficient and rely on post editing by an expert human translator. This is one area of *expert system* development.

LAP See *link access protocol.*

laptop microcomputer A portable microcomputer small enough to fit on one's lap.

large scale integration (LSI) Over 30,000 components on a single *integrated circuit.*

laser Light Amplification by the Stimulated Emission of Radiation. It is a device that emits optical radiation as a direct result of applied voltages and electron movement. The light can be pulsed on and off very rapidly and some lasers produce coherent light, *i.e.* light of a single frequency with all the waves in phase.

laser disk A *video disk* where information is read by means of a laser light beam. The data is recorded as a series of pitted tracks. As the light hits the tracks it is reflected back to a reading head that converts the variations in the reflected light into electrical signals. Optical systems such as this are not sensitive to surface contamination and there is no mechanical contact between head and disk surface to cause wear.

laser printer An *electrophotographic printer* or *xerographic printer* in which a laser is used as the light source.

laservision video disk See *laser disk.*

last in-first out (LIFO) A principle associated with accounting and computer record handling, *e.g.* the last item added to a file will be the first to be removed. A *stack* implemented in hardware is sometimes referred to as LIFO.

LC circuit An electrical network combining inductive and capacitive elements. See also *inductor* and *capacitor.*

LCD See *liquid crystal display.*

leading load A capacitive load.

leased circuit A data communication line that is leased. This ensures that the user has the private use of a line that will be cost effective for regular connections for long periods of time.

least significant bit (LSB) See *least significant character.*

least significant character In a string where the position of a character determines its significance, the least significant character is at the end of least significance. Such a string is normally written with the least significant position on the right.

least significant digit (LSD) See *least significant character.*

LED See *light emitting diode display.*

left justification Arranging lines of text so that the left hand edges are all in line. See also *right justification.*

letter quality (LQ) A type of printer output that is suitable for distribution outside an organization, *e.g.* daisy wheel printer. See also *near letter quality.*

lexigraphic order The order of words in a dictionary, following the order of letters in the alphabet.

lexigraphic sort Any sorting *algorithm* for putting items into *lexigraphic order.*

LF See *line feed/low frequency.*

library Synonymous with dictionary in some word processing applications. See also *program library, tape library.*

library loader Part of the *operating system* that inserts appropriate library routines into the *object code* ready for processing.

library routines Routines held in a system library that may be referenced within programs. See also *library loader.*

LIFO See *last in-first out.*

light emitting diode display (LED) A device used in some *calculators* and digital watches to display numerical and alphabetical characters. See also *liquid crystal display.*

light guide A glass or perspex fiber used to transfer optical signals. Light enters at one end and is totally internally reflected along the *optical fibers, i.e.* guided by the fiber.

light pen A penlike input device that is used with a *cathode ray tube* display. It can be used to point to areas on the screen and thus indicate a selection from a displayed list or it can be used to draw and manipulate shapes. The light pen has a photosensor at its tip that is able to detect the peak illumination that occurs when the CRT scanning spot passes its point of focus. A switch (usually on the pen) is used to indicate the intended start and finish of any drawing actions.

limit check A test of specified *fields* of *records* or of compound totals to determine whether certain pre-established limits have been exceeded.

line delete A function on word processing systems that allows the complete deletion of a line.

line editor An *editor* that uses line numbers for referencing a section for editing.

line ending A special character denoting the end of a short line of text, created by pressing the *carriage return* key. See also *hard return.*

line feed (LF) See also *hard return.* An instruction in a program or a button on a terminal or printer. In both cases the display or paper is moved up one line. See also *carriage return/line feed.*

line graphics A feature of some *word processors* whereby boxes can be put around text, or other horizontal and vertical lines can be drawn.

line insert To insert a blank line or lines into an existing document for presentation purposes.

line numbers Numbers denoting the start of a new line. Sometimes they act as *labels, e.g.* in the BASIC language. The program code for other languages can have line numbers assigned by the computer for cross-referencing errors and for editing.

line of sight A clear, straight, unobstructed path between two points.

line printer A printer that prints a complete line of characters at one time, and hence is generally faster than a serial or *character printer.*

line protocol A formally specified set of possible bit sequences that will guarantee that two ends of a communication link will be able to pass information between them in an understandable way. A number of standards have been devised for the implementation of such protocols, *e.g. SDLC, HDLC, ADCCP.*

line regulation A power supply's ability to eliminate, within a specified range, the output voltage deviations as the result of input line changes.

line spacing The number of lines in a vertical inch of paper. Usually specified as single or double spacing although half space and other gradations can be used.

line switching The most common form of concentration, used to connect a number of transmitting devices to a number of receiving devices. Buffering of data is done by the input devices if the transmission medium is busy. See also *concentrator.*

line telecommunications Communications that use lines, *i.e.* cables and wires, to transfer information. See also *bounded media* and *free space media.*

linear programming A technique in *optimization,* pioneered by George Dantzig, that is widely used in economic, military and business management decisions.

lines per minute (LPM) One of the terms used to describe the rate of output for a line printer.

link A path for communication that may be physical (as in a circuit) or either physical or logical (as in a channel).

Also when a field of an item contains an address for another item, a link or pointer/reference has been established.

link access protocol (LAP) The second layer (data link layer) protocol that is a subset of *HDLC* and is used in *X.25*-based networks in setting up channels between *DTE* and *DCE.*

link trials or testing Testing of a group of program modules to ensure that the modules operate correctly in combination. It is normally performed after the individual modules have been tested in isolation and prior to integration testing of the complete system.

linkage editor An operating-system program that readies programs for entrance into the core-image library.

linked files A facility that enables the operator to link a number of files together so they can be dealt with on a global basis. See also *master file.*

linked files list A data structure in which each component (cell) may be anywhere in storage. Each cell is explicitly connected to the next one by a pointer.

linked queue A queue that has a series of pointers that point to the actual data area.

linking A programming technique used to transfer control of processing to various parts of a program.

liquid crystal display (LCD) A device used in many calculators, digital watches and small computer instruments to display numerical and alphabetical characters. The power requirements are less than those for *LEDs.*

LISP See *list processing.*

listing A *printout* of the instructions contained in a *source program.*

list processing (LISP) A programming language designed for the manipulation of nonnumeric data. It is widely used in *artificial intelligence* research.

literal A word, symbol or number that describes or defines itself rather than something it might represent, *i.e.* its value is determined by its denotation.

load To copy a *file,* especially a program, from disk storage into *working storage.*

load regulation A power supply's ability to eliminate, within a specified range, the output voltage deviations as the result of load magnitude changes.

loader A *utility program* that sets up another program in *main memory* ready for execution. This usually means transferring the program from *backing store.*

local Computing capability close to the end-user.

local area network (LAN) A *communication network* linking a number of workstations in the same 'local' area. Local is variously defined as: in the same building, within a radius of 1 kilometer or within a single manufacturing plant. Such a system enables individual computers or workstations to send messages and files to each other and to share devices such as printers, *disk storage* and access to other computer systems. See also *wide area network.*

local line network The configuration of telephone line connections between subscribers and their local telephone exchange. The modern way is to connect a group of subscribers to a distribution point such as a terminal block, on a pole or wall. The distribution points are connected to small distribution or secondary cables linked to cabinets. Primary or main cables then connect the cabinets to the telephone exchange.

local variable A *variable* whose value is only accessible in a restricted part of a program. Compare *global variable.*

location See *address* and *store location.*

lock An indivisible operation that allows a process to ensure that it alone has access to a particular resource.

lockout A mechanism for arranging controlled access to a shared resource. See also *lock* and *semaphore.*

logging See *data logging.*

logging off The process by which a user indicates that he or she has finished processing on the system. Similar terms may be logoff, logout or sign off.

logging on The process by which a user identifies himself or herself to a system. Similar terms may be logon, login, logging in or sign on. This process is usually required for *multi-user systems* where the number of users accessing the system needs to be controlled and/or *security checks* are made.

logic The science of reasoning, proof, thinking or inference.

logic circuit The basic building blocks of digital electronics often referred to as *logic gates.*

logic gate A device, usually electronic, that implements an elementary logic function such as *AND, OR, NAND, NOR* and *NOT.*

logic seeking A characteristic of printers that effectively skip over any blank spaces in text, thereby achieving much faster printing speeds.

logic symbols A set of graphic symbols that express the function of individual *logic gates* in a logic diagram.

logical operation A mathematical process based on the principles of *truth tables.* See also *AND, OR* and *NAND.*

logical operator An *operator* used for denoting a logical function, *e.g. AND, OR, NAND, NOR, NOT.*

login See *logging on.*

LOGO A programming language with list processing features, widely known for *turtle graphics.*

logoff See *logging off.*

logon See *logging on.*

logout See *logging off.*

LOGO A programming language with list processing features, widely known for *turtle graphics.*

longitudinal record check A *parity check* performed on the bits in each track of a block of recorded data on magnetic tape or paper tape.

lookup table See *table lookup.*

loop A sequence of *instructions* in a program; the sequence is repeated until some specific condition occurs.

loosely coupled system A *multiprocessing system* in which the central processors cannot communicate rapidly.

low frequency (LF) A band of radio frequencies between 30kHz and 300kHz, usually used for long wave transmissions.

low level programming language A variety of programming languages in which the control and data structures directly reflect the underlying *machine architecture.*

low resolution graphics A term generally applied to graphical display units where simple pictures can be built up by plotting relatively large blocks of color or by using special graphic characters. See also *resolution.*

lowercase The small letters in typefaces (uncapitalized letters such as *a, b, c,* etc.).

LPM See *lines per minute.*

LQ See *letter quality.*

LSB Least significant bit. See *least significant character.*

LSI See *large scale integration.*

M

M See *mega-*.

m See *milli-*.

machine architecture The specification of a digital computer system at a general level.

machine code The *operation code* of a particular machine.

machine cycle The length of time required for the computer to perform one machine operation.

machine independence A software design philosophy allowing programs written on one type of computer to be run without changes on another type of computer.

machine intelligence See *artificial intelligence.*

machine language The written representation of *machine code.*

machine-oriented language A language in which there is a general one-to-one correspondence between *source-program* statements and operations performed by the computer.

machine timing The regular cycle of events in the operation of internal microprocessor circuitry.

machine tool control See *numerical control.*

macro Short for *macro instruction.*

macro instruction An instruction in a programming language that causes several instructions of the same language to be generated, and which is replaced by those instructions in the program. This is usually a feature of *low level programming languages.*

magnetic bubble memory See *bubble memory.*

magnetic card A data medium consisting of a card that is partly or completely coated on one side with ferromagnetic film on which data can be encoded and read, *e.g.* credit card.

magnetic cell A memory element in which two different states of its magnetic flux pattern are used to represent binary values. The element may be part of a ferromagnetic core or the intersection of two coated wires and it can store one single bit of information.

magnetic disk A storage device consisting of a flat rotatable circular plate coated with a magnetic material. Data is input to or read from a set of concentric tracks. See also *disk* and *magnetic media.*

magnetic drum The earliest form of rotating magnetic storage. It is a cylindrical storage device, the outside surface of which is coated with a magnetic material. Some of the first computers used magnetic drums as main memory devices because other forms of random access store were volatile, bulky and expensive.

magnetic encoding The method by which binary data is recorded on magnetic media.

magnetic ink Ink containing ferromagnetic particles that is used to print characters which will be subsequently read by *MICR* devices.

magnetic ink character reading device (MICR) Magnetic read heads that interpret data printed in magnetic ink.

The most common application is reading encoded numbers on the bottom of bank checks.

magnetic media The various types of media on which data recording is effected by writing a magnetic pattern onto the magnetizable surface of the medium, *e.g.* magnetic tapes, magnetic disks, magnetic cards.

magnetic storage device See *magnetic media.*

magnetic strip card A card that contains some conventionally printed or typed information and a magnetic strip for encoding data. See *magnetic card.*

magnetic strip reader An input device that reads the information encoded on a magnetic strip, *e.g. credit card.*

magnetic tape An information storage medium consisting of flexible tape with a magnetic coating. See also *magnetic media.*

magnetic tape unit (MTU) The peripheral device upon which magnetic tapes are placed for reading. Also called tape transport, tape drive, tape deck and tape mechanism.

magnetographic printer A type of printer in which the required image is first written on a band or drum of magnetic recording material as a pattern of closely spaced poles. The image is then developed by brushing it with a pigment that is ferromagnetic and thermoplastic. The image is transferred and bonded to paper by applying pressure and/or heat.

magneto-optic disk A storage device using the magneto-optic effect where a laser beam and a magnetic field are applied to a small area of the disk to write information. The disk is scanned by polarized light to read the information. This technique has the potential for achieving recording densities many times higher than conventional magnetic encoding.

mail box The destination, often secure, for documents or data that have been transmitted via an *electronic mail* system.

mail handling equipment Equipment used for handling manual mail items, including machines for letter opening, addressing, envelope sealing, inserting and folding, rolling and wrapping, tucking and folding, franking.

mail merge A *word processing* function which combines standard form text with *variable text* to produce personalized documents.

mail order system A computer system designed to provide the processing requirements for a company that accepts orders by mail or telephone and deals with the customer directly, not via retail shops.

main memory See *main store.*

main storage The memory of the computer that can be accessed immediately. *Core store* and *solid state devices* are used for the main store while magnetic tape and disks are used for *backing store.*

mainframe computer Generally the combination of *central processor* and primary memory of a computer system. However the term is frequently used to refer to any large computer system.

maintenance The process of preventive work to avoid possible hardware or software failures, or remedial work to correct any faults that have already occurred.

maintenance contract Most computer manufacturers and equipment suppliers offer service contracts to include regular preventive maintenance and terms for guaranteed call-out times.

management information system (MIS) An information system whose prime purpose is to supply information to managers. Early MIS systems were designed by *systems analysts* to provide the information requirements of individual managers within an organization. The information would be supplied routinely or on demand to meet certain prespecified needs.

management support in the electronic office This component of electronic office facilities includes electronic in-tray, *diary management,* scheduling options, reminder files and electronically controlled communications for voice and mail.

man-machine interface (MMI) Man-machine interaction is the study of communication requirements between man and machine. An interface is the link that enables a machine to understand the requirements of a human, *i.e.* different *input devices* such as *graphics, icon* systems, handheld *mouse, natural language* and voice contact; or a human to understand the resulting output from a machine, *i.e. printers, plotters, screens, voice output* and any equipment that will respond to an electrical signal.

mantissa See *floating point* and *normalization of data.*

manufacturing system See *computer integrated manufacturing.*

MAR See *memory address register.*

margin The physical boundary of text, on the left and right side of a screen or page.

margination The capability of word processing systems to set margins automatically by specifying where lines begin and end in relation to the width of the paper.

mark (block) To identify a specific portion of text by putting *block* markers at the beginning and end of the piece of text, for special editing during word processing.

mark sense reader An input device that reads special forms (or cards), usually by electrically sensing the marks in predetermined positions. Initially the marks were made with soft graphite pencils to provide good electrical conductivity. Now most systems use photoelectrical sensing techniques.

marker See *BOT marker* and *end of tape.*

marketing support Liaison activity between a vendor/supplier and users.

mask An overlay technique for modifying or identifying a part of a *byte* or *word.* A bit pattern, the same length as the item to be masked, is generated and stored as a mask. By use of appropriate logical operators such as AND, the mask can be used to suppress bits in the data or set them to zero.

mass storage An *on-line backing store* system capable of storing larger quantities of data than conventional backing store, *e.g. automated tape libraries.*

master file (1) A file of records that is the principal source of information for a job. (2) In word processing, a file that is interpreted by the program to include a number of smaller files. The master file feature of some word processing programs allows the operator to define formats for a large book-length document but work on files of more manageable size such as chapters for entry and editing purposes.

matrix A two-dimensional *array.*

matrix output See *dot matrix printer.*

matrix printer See *dot matrix printer.*

MATS See *mobile automatic telephone system.*

MB See *megabyte.*

MBR See *memory buffer register.*

MDR See *memory data register.*

mean time between failures (MTBF) The probable length of time that a component taken from a particular batch will survive if operated under the same conditions as a sample from that particular batch. It provides a quantitative assessment for component (or system) reliability. See also *confidence level.*

media In information processing, vehicles for storing information. See also *data medium.*

medium frequency- (MF) A range of radio waves used for sound broadcasting with frequencies between 300kHz and 3MHz.

medium scale integration (MSI) Up to a hundred components on an *integrated circuit.*

mega- (M) The prefix to a unit indicating a multiple of one million, *e.g.* 1×10^6 bytes is a megabyte.

megabyte (MB) One million *bytes.*

memory A device or medium that can retain information for subsequent retrieval. The term is synonymous with storage and store, although it is most frequently used for referring to the internal storage of a computer that can be directly addressed by *operating instructions.*

memory address register (MAR) The central processor *register* that holds the address of the next *store location* to be referenced.

memory buffer register (MBR) The central processor *register* that acts as a *buffer* for all data transfers to and from *main store.*

memory data register (MDR) A central processor *register* for holding information (either program words or data words) that is in the process of being transferred from the memory to the central processor, or vice versa.

memory device See *storage device.*

memory dump A representation, which can be read by a person, of the contents of the main memory of a computer system at a specific time. A memory dump is usually taken for *postmortem* analysis.

memory location See *store location.*

memory management Control of the memory structure of a system as a whole or the control of allocation of individual parts of the memory as required by the different processes taking place.

memory map A schematic presentation of the use to which memory is being put, often produced as a by-product during the compilation of a program.

memory switching system A communications system that uses a computer to accept messages from its terminals, store if necessary, and then transmit them to other terminals as indicated by the message.

memory typewriter A typewriter that can store up to 200,000 characters and instructions about line spacing, headings, etc. Individual documents are named when they are filed. See also *electronic typewriter.*

memory unit See *memory.*

menu A displayed list of processing options from which a choice can be made.

merge To combine two or more ordered files into a single ordered file.

merged transistor logic (MTL) Another name for *integrated injection logic.*

message switching A data switching strategy that does not require a physical path between sender and receiver before communication can take place. Messages are passed via relays called switching offices in a *store and forward system.* The term is also used informally for *packet switching.*

metalanguage A language used to describe a programming language.

metal-oxide semiconductor field effect transistor (MOSFET) A type of *field effect transistor* that has an insulating layer of oxide, usually silicon oxide, separating the gate from the drain-source conduction channel in the semiconductor.

MF See *medium frequency.*

MICR Magnetic ink character recognition. See *magnetic ink character reading device.*

micro See *microcomputer.*

micro- A prefix to a unit indicating a submultiple of one million, *e.g.* 1×10^{-6} seconds is a microsecond.

microcircuit An *integrated circuit,* generally performing a very complex function, *e.g.* a *microprocessor* composed of arithmetic and logic unit, control circuits, *registers,* program counter and some memory, all within a single integrated circuit.

microcomputer A computer system that utilizes a *microprocessor* as its central control and arithmetic element.

microelectronics That section of electronics that uses extremely small electronic parts, *e.g. integrated circuits.*

microfiche An output medium consisting of large capacity *microfilm* sheets (sometimes card mounted), which may be randomly accessed by special optical readers/magnifiers. See also *computer output microfilm* and *microforms*.

microfilm Rolls of photographic film that hold copies of documents. Often microfiche are used in preference to microfilm. See also *microforms.*

microforms A method of storage, retrieval and display of images recorded on microfilm. Other names include micro-image, micrographics, optical storage and computer fiche. The computer may be used to generate an index of images, relate index contents to a particular roll or fiche of film and retrieve images via index retrieval and search methods.

micrographics The storage of documents onto a type of *microform,* such as microfiche or microfilm, by a process of photographic miniaturization.

micro-image See *microforms.*

microinstructions See *microprogramming.*

microprocessor A miniature computer contained on a single integrated circuit.

microprocessor unit (MPU) The primary control and arithmetic element of a microcomputer system.

microprogram store The memory that contains a microprogram. It may be fixed (ROM) or alterable. See also *microprogramming.*

microprogramming A method of carrying out the *control unit* functions by describing the steps in that function as a sequence of operations that are much more elementary than *instructions*. In this method of designing and building a control unit, an additional memory, commonly called a microprogram store, contains a sequence of microinstructions.

Microsoft BASIC A dialect of *BASIC* that has become the de facto standard of the microcomputer industry.

microwave communication *Radio transmission* at very high frequencies that enables thousands of *multiplexed* voice channels to be carried between terminals.

microwaves Electromagnetic waves similar to radio waves but at a different frequency.

microwriter A portable device with a six-key keyboard, one line display and a memory. Different combinations of the keys provide a full character set so that letters, notes and reports may be written, stored and edited while out of the office, *e.g.* on a train or plane, for subsequent transfer to a *word processor.*

milli- (m) A prefix to a unit indicating a submultiple of one thousand, *e.g.* 1×10^{-3} seconds is a millisecond.

mini See *minicomputer.*

minicomputer Originally a computer that physically fit within a single equipment cabinet, it was cheaper and slower with smaller memory and word size than a *mainframe computer*. The term predates the *microcomputer* and the boundary between these two classes of devices is not precise.

minidiskette See *floppy disk.*

minifloppy See *floppy disk.*

MIPS An abbreviation for million instructions per second, a measure of computer power.

MIS See *management information system.*

MMI See *man-machine interface.*

mnemonics Memory aids frequently used to simplify commands, often by using related letters in place of words; *e.g.*, *p* for *print.*

mnemonic code A simple form of *assembly language,* the name is derived from the use of mnemonic abbreviations for operation codes, *e.g.* LDA for 'load accumulator.'

mobile automatic telephone system (MATS) The provision of a nationwide facility for mobile subscribers (in a car or train) to have their own individual numbers so they can operate in a way similar to the normal line-fed telephone. This is now possible with *cellular radio* systems.

mobile radio system See *cellular radio.*

mode A general term used in many contexts concerning the methods of operation and use of a computer system, *e.g. conversational mode* refers to *interactive terminal* use.

modeling To create a computer model of a physical or theoretical system in order to examine the effect of different parameter changes, *e.g.* civil engineering structures, aircraft models, chemical reaction processes, cash forecasts, business conditions and economic trends.

modem A device that can convert a *digital signal* of bits into an *analog signal* of electrical impulses for transmission over telephone-type circuits and vice versa.

modular programming An aspect of *structured programming* in which individual tasks are programmed in distinct sections or modules. One advantage is the ease with which individual sections can be modified without reference to other sections.

modulation The technique of using *data signals* to modify a transmitted carrier wave so that the wave carries the data signals. The three ways of altering a wave are: changing its *amplitude,* changing its *frequency* or changing its *phase.*

modulator-demodulator (MODEM) See *modem.*

module A section or segment of a *program* that can be independently changed. See also *modular programming.*

monitor A program similar to an operating system which allows the user of a small system to write simple programs, debug programs, and test a microcomputer's capabilities.

monolithic IC An integrated circuit made from one material, *e.g.* a silicon wafer.

monomode optical fibers *Optical fibers* with very small diameters that provide only a single mode of transmission. Compare *multimode optical fibers.*

monoprogramming system A name given to the traditional batch system whereby one user program is loaded and totally executed before the next user program can be brought into the memory.

monospacing A method of printing in which each character takes up the same amount of space horizontally, irrespective of the size of character. Compare *proportional spacing.*

monostable multivibrator See *multivibrator.*

most significant bit (MSB) See *most significant character.*

most significant character The character in the most significant position in a number, word, signal, etc. In a string where the position of a character determines its significance, the most significant character is at the end of most significance. Such a string is normally written with the most significant position on the left.

most significant digit (MSD) See *most significant character.*

mother board A *printed circuit* board that holds the principal components in a *microcomputer* system.

mouse A device that is moved by the hand to indicate a precise position on a digital data tablet. The data tablet and associated processor can correlate the function indicated by the switches on the mouse with the precise position on the tablet.

move block To remove a marked block of text from one location in a document, and reposition it at another location during word processing.

movement file See *transaction file.*

MPU See *microprocessor unit.*

MSB Most significant bit. See *most significant character.*

MSD Most significant digit. See *most significant character.*

MS-DOS An *operating system* for IBM-compatible systems.

MSI See *medium scale integration.*

MSR Marketing support representative. The vendor's representative for training and assistance in using word processing and computer equipment.

MTBF See *mean time between failures.*

MTL See *merged transistor logic.*

MTU See *magnetic tape unit.*

multiaccess system A system allowing several users to make apparently simultaneous use of a computer. Each user has a terminal and is connected via a *multiplexor* or *front end processor* to the main system. See also *time sharing.*

multiboard computer A computer requiring several circuit boards to complete the system, *e.g.* boards for the input/output interface, ROM and RAM boards, microprocessor board, graphics board, etc. They are all mounted on the *mother board.*

multicasting A generalization of *broadcasting* in which special address *flags* are used to indicate that particular messages are of interest to particular classes of *nodes*, but not necessarily all the nodes on the network.

multichannel recording system A system of recording dialog among multioriginators using individual microphones which record onto separate tracks of magnetic tape.

multifunction workstation A workstation from which a variety of different tasks can be carried out.

multimedia mail A form of mail that can combine text, graphics, voice, facsimile and other forms of information in a single message. See also *electronic mail.*

multimode optical fibers Thick core *optical fibers* with many possible modes of transmission. Compare *monomode optical fibers.*

multipart stationery Boxes of continuous paper supplied as sheets interleaved with carbon paper ready to provide multiple copies of printed output.

multiple precision arithmetic A system of logic in which the microcomputer uses two or more *words* to represent one number.

multiple processing Using two or more *microprocessors* in a single system, operating out of common *memory,* permitting execution of many programs.

multiplexer A device which takes a number of *channels* and combines the signals into one common channel for transmission.

multiplexing The process of combining multiple messages simultaneously on the same physical or logical transmission medium.

multiprocessing system A system in which more than one processor may be active at any one time. See also *multiprogramming system.*

multiprocessor A computer system that consists of multiple *central processors* that can access part or all of the aggregate resources of the system.

multiprogramming operating system An operating system that executes multiple programs concurrently.

multiprogramming system A system in which several individual programs may be active. Each active program implies a running process, but only one process runs at any one time on any particular processor. It is feasible to run a multiprogramming system on a single processor. A multiprocessor system will also be a multiprogramming system.

multistrike ribbon A type of carbon ribbon that lasts longer than an ordinary (single strike) ribbon, since it can withstand several passes through the printer.

multitask system A computer system that is capable of performing a number of different tasks apparently simultaneously.

multitasking The concurrent execution of a number of tasks, *i.e.* of a number of jobs or processes. See also *parallel processing.*

multitasking capability The ability to perform more than one task at the same time.

multiterminal system A system capable of providing facilities for several terminals.

multiuser system See *multiprocessing system* and *multiprogramming system.*

multivibrator An electronic oscillator, it is a basic electronic circuit that can be built using two transistors and a few components. The astable multivibrator continuously switches from one of its two states to the other and is used in computers as a clock. The bistable multivibrator rests in one or the other of its two states and is used to store a binary digit (sometimes known as a 'flip-flop'). The monostable multivibrator, once switched to the other state, always reverts to its first state after a fixed time and is used for fixed timing or as a delay circuit.

multiwindow The ability of a screen to display more than one document or task. See also *window.*

music synthesizer An output device that generates sounds similar to musical notes upon the receipt of digital signals.

MX queue In MP/M, a mutual-exclusion queue that can be used to control serially reusable resources such as a printer. See *queue.*

N

n See *nano-*.

NAND function This function combines statements such that the outcome will be true (1) for all combinations of true (1) and false (0) statements except when they are all true (1).

NAND gate An electronic logic device that performs according to the *NAND function, i.e.* it corresponds to the logical operation of NOT(p AND q), and the output signal will be 1 for all combinations of 1 and 0 except when all input signals are 1.

nano- (n) A prefix to a unit indicating a submultiple of one thousand million, *e.g.* 1×10^{-9} seconds is a nanosecond.

narrowband A telecommunications channel with low capacity. See also bandwidth and *wideband networks.*

National Television Systems Committee (NTSC) The committee responsible for the NTSC system of television developed and introduced in the U.S.A. in the early 1950s, and later adopted by Canada, Japan and Mexico.

natural binary coded decimal (NBCD) See *binary coded decimal.*

natural language A language existing by nature (such as English) and not created artificially.

NBCD Natural binary coded decimal. See *binary coded decimal.*

NC See *numerical control.*

near letter quality (NLQ) Printer output that is not as good as letter quality but still acceptable for most purposes.

negation (1) In arithmetic, the operation of changing the sign of a nonzero arithmetic quantity, *e.g.* 3 to −3 and −10 to 10. Negation is usually denoted by the minus sign. (2) In logic, the application of the *NOT function* on a statement, truth value or formula.

NEQ function The nonequivalence function combines statements such that the outcome will be false (0) if all statements are true (1) or all statements are false (0), otherwise the outcome will be true (1). It is also known as the exclusive-OR function.

NEQ gate The nonequivalence electronic logic device that performs according to the *NEQ function, i.e.* it provides a logic value of 0 when all its input values are the same. It is also known as the exclusive-OR gate.

network In communications, a loosely defined term applied to any system consisting of terminals, *nodes* and interconnecting media. In general, a network is a collection of resources used to establish and switch communication paths between its terminals. The interconnections can include *line telecommunications, trunks, satellites, microwave communications* and medium/long wave *radio transmissions.*

network analysis An operational research technique where each activity in a process is mapped on a diagram that indicates which tasks may be carried out in parallel and which must be processed in sequence. This activity chart provides a link between activities and details of times required to complete each activity. The network provides a critical path consisting of those activities that must be completed on time in order not to delay the total project.

network architecture The design and implementation of a communication network with respect to its communication disciplines and its interconnection topology. It deals explicitly with the encoding of information, its transmission, error control, flow control, techniques for addressing subscribers on a network and analysis of network performance under abnormal or degraded conditions.

network data base system A data base management system based on the concept of ownership. Member records are 'owned' by owner records and each member record type may have a number of owner record types. Compare with *hierarchical communication system.*

network diagrams See *network analysis.*

network processor A name given to one type of *multiplexor* that includes a *minicomputer* or *microcomputer* to improve the utilization of transmission lines. Other names include data concentrator and statistical multiplexers.

neutral The junction point of the legs in a *wye* circuit.

nibble A sequence of 4 bits operated upon as a unit.

NLQ See *near letter quality.*

node A connection point or junction in a network where two or more devices are linked together. Nodes can also be called *stations* and in many *X.25* networks the switching nodes are called *exchanges.*

noise This is any signal that occurs in an electronic or communication system that is extraneous to the signal being propagated.

noise immunity The measure of the amount of *noise* that a circuit can tolerate without producing errors.

noise margin The maximum *noise* voltage that can be added to or subtracted from a logic signal before a threshold voltage for a logic state is passed.

nonfriction feed The process of pulling *continuous form paper* through a printer, usually accomplished by a built-in or a detachable forms tractor.

nonimpact printer A printer in which the image is formed without the use of mechanical impact, *e.g. ink jet, thermal* and *xerographic printers.*

nonvolatile memory Types of memory whose contents are not lost when the power is switched off, *e.g. ROM, PROM* and *core store.* Compare with *volatile memory.*

nonvolatile store See *nonvolatile memory.*

NOR function This function combines statements such that the outcome will only be true (1) if all statements are false (0).

NOR gate An electronic logic device that performs according to the *NOR function, i.e.* it corresponds to the logical operation of NOT(p OR q) when the output signal will be 1 only when all input signals are 0.

normalization of data The process of converting data into a specific form for computer use. This results in numbers being held in two parts, the fraction or mantissa holds the significant digits and the exponent or characteristic indicates where the decimal point must be placed in order to arrive back at the original number.

NOT function This function works upon a single statement to reverse its state, *i.e.* true (1) to false (0) and vice versa.

NOT gate An electronic logic device that performs according to the *NOT function.* It is sometimes known as an 'inverter' because the output is always the opposite of the input.

NTSC See *National Television Systems Committee.*

n-type material Semiconductor materials with an increased number of electrons. ('N' means more negative.) The conductivity of a material such as silicon can be changed by the addition of a small amount of an impurity such as arsenic which increases the number of electrons. See also *p-type material.*

nucleus That part of an *operating system* that is the center of all control and resource-management activities.

null character A special character in a character set, denoting nothing, and usually represented by zero. (As in *ASCII* and *EBCDIC.)*

null list An empty list.

null string Another name for an empty *string.*

number cruncher A name given to a computer, usually a large, *mainframe computer,* whose task is to carry out large mathematical calculations. An informal name for a *supercomputer.*

numeric A term defining a field, variable, etc., that must only contain a valid number.

numeric keypad A small keyboard that only has keys with numerals on it (often in addition to the row of number keys found on a standard keyboard).

numerical analysis A branch of mathematics dealing with the numerical solution of problems formulated and studied in other branches of mathematics. Numerical analysis now plays an important part in engineering and in the quantitative parts of pure and applied science. On the practical side it involves writing efficient and reliable computer routines for a wide variety of problems.

numerical control (NC) The application of digital computer techniques to the control of a manufacturing process. Generally techniques are linked to controlling tools such as milling, welding, metal cutting and other specialized machine tools.

O

OA See *office automation.*

object code The output of a *compiler.*

object program A program that is the result of a translation process.

OCCAM A language developed in order to program *transputers* that are working together.

OCR See *optical character recognition.*

octal number system The representation of numbers as multiples of 8. The octal digits are denoted by 0 to 7, *e.g.* digital 8 is octal 10, digital 12 is octal 14.

octal scale See *octal number system.*

odd parity A property that holds when a group of binary values contains an odd number of *1s.*

off-line A device is said to be off-line when connected to a system but unavailable for use. Compare *on-line.*

office automation (OA) The application of computers to office tasks. See also *electronic office.*

office copier See *photocopier.*

office system See *electronic office.*

OMR Optical mark reading. See *mark sense reader.*

on-line Having to do with operations carried out on word processing/computer equipment directly under control of the system's *central processing unit.*

on-line system A computer system having inline processing capabilities which can be provided only when a system has online input/output devices.

on-line transaction processing See *transaction processing.*

one's complement The one's complement of a binary number is that binary number which, when added to the original number, will produce all *1s*, *e.g.* the one's complement of 1011 is 0100.

OP-AMP See *operational amplifier.*

op-code See *operation code.*

open a file To reserve storage space on the disk for a new file.

open access facilities Providing computer workstations for general use, at any time, with suitable supervision. (Primarily computer provisioning requirements for education.)

open system A network deliberately built to standards that enable different types and makes of systems to be interconnected.

open system interconnection (OSI) A concept whereby communication oriented computer equipment with different *protocols* can be interconnected by means of a data network.

operand A quantity or function upon which a mathematical or logical operation is performed.

operating instructions *Instructions* for operating a computer system.

operating system (OS) The set of software products that jointly control the system resources and the processes using these resources in a computer system.

operating system software See *operating system.*

operating temperature The temperature range in which a power supply will operate and maintain all of its specified characteristics.

operation code (op-code) The portion of the *instruction* word that specifies the operation to be performed by the instruction.

operation schedules The name given to daily, weekly or monthly schedules of work for the computer operations staff.

operation trial A system trial that checks not only programs but also data preparation and all related manual systems.

operational amplifier (OP-AMP) A very high gain voltage amplifier having a differential input, *i.e.* its output voltage is proportional to (and very much greater than) the voltage difference between its two inputs.

operational information Information relating to the day-to-day running of each business.

operational research (OR) The study of some human operation or set of operations by quantitative means. It is usually conducted with the aid of computer *modeling;* models may be hypothesized and fitted to experimental data or experimental data may be analyzed to derive a model. Once a model is available, the effects of changes in the operations under study can be developed and predicted in a quantitative way.

operator (1) A person responsible for operating and interacting with specific equipment, *e.g.* computer operator, word processing operator. (2) A symbol interpreted by a computer program, such as BASIC, as an instruction to perform one of the elementary arithmetic operations, *e.g.* + for addition, / for division or ^ for raising to a power.

operator precedence The sequence by which the computer will evaluate an expression when there are a number of different operations. First any items in brackets will be evaluated, then, in order of priority, operations with ^ , * or /, + or −, and =.

operator's console A special terminal reserved for operator use. System and job commands will be keyed in and any special messages for the operator will be displayed.

operator's log A list of operator activities including records of errors and problems encountered during the work shift. The operator may be controlling a computer system or working at an individual workstation.

optical character recognition (OCR) The process in which a machine, using light sensing methods, scans, recognizes and encodes information printed or typed in stylized characters. Commercial and business organizations make use of specially preprinted characters on documents frequently. See also *turnaround document.*

optical communication system A communication system that exploits light as the carrier of information (in contrast to electrical signals). See also *optical fibers.*

optical disk A high-capacity, random-access disk providing WORM (write once, read many) storage. Digital data is stored in the form of microscopic pits (representing bits) burned into the disk by a laser. Data is retrieved by a laser reader.

optical fibers Fibers made from special glass or plastic that enable light to be transmitted along their length by means of repeated internal reflections. As two different types of glass are used, the total internal reflection involves very little energy loss.

optical font A printing *font* or style of character specially designed to be accurately read by reading machines and by people.

optical mark reading (OMR) See *mark sense reader.*

optical storage See *microforms.*

optimization The process of finding the best solution to some problem, where 'best' meets a set of defined criteria.

OR See *operational research.*

OR function This function combines statements such that the outcome is only false (0) if all statements are false (0); otherwise the outcome is true (1).

OR gate An electronic device that performs according to the *OR function, i.e.* all inputs must be 0 to obtain an output of 0.

Oracle The name of the IBA's *teletext* service that transmits data along with normal television programs transmissions. A teletext decoder is required in addition to the normal television receiver.

organization chart A chart that presents the structure of an organization in the form of groups of people within departments, indicating line functions and responsibilities.

originator The writer or author of a document.

orphan line The last line of a paragraph that appears by itself at the top of a page. See also *widow line.*

OS See *operating system.*

OSI See *open system interconnection.*

OS/2 The operating system for the new generation of IBM personal computers, called the PS/2 series.

outline system This is the initial design for a new system that would be prepared during a *feasibility study.*

output The result of some information processing activity. It might be produced on printed paper, as a screen dis play or as a signal to control another device or activity.

output device Any device that converts electrical signals, representing information within a computer, into a form that can exist or be sensed outside the computer, *e.g. printers, VDUs, plotters* and *voice synthesis.*

output file A file containing some results from processing, often created for printing and archiving.

output stream An output channel, *e.g.* all output is directed to a specific line printer.

overflow The condition that arises when the result of an arithmetic operation exceeds the size of the number variable allotted for receipt of that result.

overlapped processing A technique whereby reading, writing and internal processing can occur simultaneously.

overlay A section of code that is loaded into memory during the execution of a program, overwriting the previous code. Overlaying is a facility for overcoming a problem of memory shortage.

overstrike The function of a hard-copy printer to strike a character more than once, producing a boldface effect.

over-under short The deviation of a power supply's output following, and as the result of, a dynamic load or line change.

over-voltage protection The circuit that monitors output voltage and causes a power supply to shut down or shorts the output if the output voltage exceeds a predetermined value.

overwrite To write or store information on top of and replacing previous information.

P

p See *pico-*.

PABX See *private automatic branch exchange.*

package See *application packages.*

packaged software Software which is designed, multi-copied, packaged, and sold through retail stores, agents, etc.

packed data See *packed decimal.*

packed decimal An economical method of storing decimal digits represented as *binary coded decimals,* using only four bits per digit.

packet A group of bits of fixed maximum size and well defined format that is switched and transmitted as a composite whole through a *packet switched network.* Any message exceeding the maximum size is partitioned and carried as several packets.

packet network See *packet switched data service.*

packet radio A transmission method that makes use of radio broadcast signals carrying *packets* of data.

packet switched data service (PSDS) A national or international data transmission service that utilizes *packet switching* techniques.

packet switched network See *packet switched data service.*

packet switching A communications technique that divides long messages into short *packets* of fixed maximum length.

packing density A measure of the quantity of data that can be held per unit of length or area on a *storage medium*. Also used to refer to the number of electronic devices per unit area of one *integrated circuit.*

padding A filler used to extend a *string* or record to some prescribed length.

page The unit of interchange between memory and *swapping device* involved in a *paging system.* Also the amount of text that a piece of paper holds or that is contained in a screen display.

page break A code that is inserted, either by an operator or the system, during *pagination* in word processing. When the printer encounters a page break, it ejects the paper, a new sheet is fed in and then printing is resumed. With continuous stationery, it leaves a space on each side of the perforation.

page display The name given to a word processing *display format* in which between 50 and 70 lines of text can be displayed on the screen.

page length A parameter that can be adjusted in word processing systems.

page printer A type of printer that prints a complete page of output in one cycle. It is generally a *nonimpact printer.* Compare *line printer* and *serial printer.*

page zero The memory page that includes the lowest-numbered memory address.

pagination The process of breaking text up into units that will fit on a given size of page. See also *page break.*

paging The transfer of *pages* of data or instructions between main memory and backing storage.

paging system A method of managing *virtual storage.* The logical address is subdivided into two fields representing the word or byte within a page and the particular page. Active pages are held in memory and a page that is not active may be transferred to the *swapping device.*

paper slew A rapid and continuous movement of paper in a line printer such that the space of several line pitches occurs without printing. In high performance line printers, the throw rate may be 75 inches per second (190 cm/s). See also *form feed.*

paper tape A data medium in the form of continuous tape of paper with uniform width and thickness.

paper tape equipment Reader and punch equipment used for data entry via paper tape and data output onto paper tape.

parallel computer A computer that is capable of *parallel processing.*

parallel data transmission Bits composing a character are sent simultaneously along separate data lines. Compare *serial data transmission.*

parallel input/output (PIO) See *parallel data transmission.*

parallel input, parallel output (PIPO) A method of data transfer where a device may receive and send data as parallel input streams for each bit within a *word.* Compare *serial input, serial output.*

parallel input, serial output (PISO) A method of data transfer where a device may receive data as parallel input streams for each bit within a word and transfer output data into a sequential stream of bits. Compare *serial input, parallel output.*

parallel interface A peripheral *interface* to the *CPU* by way of the *system bus* that sends or receives data in parallel from another computer or device.

parallel operation Two or more units of the same *voltage* connected together to obtain a higher *current* than would be available from a single unit. Sometimes *diode* isolation is included to produce *redundancy* in critical applications.

parallel processing Processing where more than one particular process is active at any given time. The term is only correctly used when more than one processor is active among a group of processes at any one instant.

parallel running When an old (manual or computer) system is used at the same time as a new system for final testing and comparison of results and performance. Also the term parallel running can be used instead of *parallel processing.*

parallel transmission See *parallel data transmission.*

parameter The name or value made available to a subprogram, *e.g.* subroutine or procedure, from a calling program or vice versa.

parity bit A check bit that is generated to verify the accuracy of *binary* values. The parity bit is zero if the number of 1's in the original group of bits was even, and it is one if the number of 1's in the original group of bits was odd.

parity check When a *binary* value is read the bit group is checked, the *parity bit* calculated and then compared with the existing parity bit.

parity error An error which is detected when the number of bits in a set of data, *e.g.* a byte or a word, have an odd (even) sum for even (odd) parity.

parity track The track on a magnetic tape or *paper tape* that is used to hold the *parity bit.*

parsing The process of deciding whether a string of input symbols is a sentence of a given language.

part page display The name given to a *display format* in which between 16 and 24 lines of text can be displayed on the screen. This is the most common display format in word processing systems.

partition A *memory* segment in a *multiprogramming* system into which an application can be loaded.

PASCAL A high level language designed as a tool to assist the teaching of programming as a systematic discipline. It has been implemented on a range of computers including microcomputers.

password A commonly used method of authenticating a user's identification. It is usually a sequence of characters that must be presented to the computer system at *login* time before access is permitted to either application software or specific files.

patch A change to a program, usually to correct an error, that is introduced in a manner that emphasizes convenience and speed of change rather than security, and is intended as a temporary repair.

patchboard A matrix of sockets that can be interconnected manually by means of patchcords, *i.e.* cables with plugs attached to each end. Patchcords are cables used to make temporary connections between devices, to program *analog computers* and to connect different peripheral devices to computer lines.

pattern recognition The process of recognizing the presence of a specified pattern in a signal or assigning a probability to its possible presence. Pattern recognition employs techniques of *digital signal processing, picture processing* and *artificial intelligence.*

PAX See *private automatic exchange.*

PBX Private branch exchange. A telephone system with internal and external calls that require operator intervention for connection.

PC See *personal computer.*

PCB Printed circuit board. See *printed circuit.*

PDL See *program design language.*

peek An instruction to examine the contents of an absolute memory location from a high level language, usually by means of a function whose argument is the address in question. Compare *poke.*

peripheral Any device, including *I/O devices* and *backing store,* that is connected to a computer. See *PIP.*

peripheral interface adapter (PIA) A set of electronic circuits fitted to a processor or a peripheral to achieve compatibility between the *interfaces.*

permanent error An irrecoverable error on a magnetic tape system. Compare *transient error.*

personal computer (PC) A general purpose single user *microcomputer* designed to be operated by one person at a time. Personal computers range from inexpensive domestic or hobby machines with limited memory, program storage on cassette or floppy disk using a TV as the display device, to extremely sophisticated machines with powerful processors, large capacity disk storage, high resolution color graphics and many other options. In industry and commerce, the personal computer is a real alternative to a terminal, especially since communication *ports* allow transfers of data between personal computers and other computers.

personal identification device (PID) A device that is entered into a terminal to establish the holder as an authorized user of the system. They are sometimes used in connection with a *PIN*.

personal identification number (PIN) A number allocated to the user of an on-line computer system. The number is unique and must be entered into the system by the user as a means of establishing the user's identity. It is often used in conjunction with a *password* and may also be part of a card or key *PID*.

petal printer See *daisy wheel printer.*

phase The stage of development of a quantity, *e.g.* two sinusoidal waves of the same *frequency* will be in phase if they both reach their peak at the same time.

phased changeover See *pilot operation.*

phone charge card A special card for use with the various telephone companies. It is encoded with information about the number of phone call units that may be used.

photocopier A machine that makes paper copies of keyed or printed pages using a photographic process.

photoelectric cell A device that responds to light by generating an electrical current.

phototypesetting A computer controlled system for producing publication quality print from initial text, ready for subsequent printing.

PIA See *peripheral interface adapter.*

pica The name of a printing pitch in which 10 characters are printed to the horizontal inch.

pico- (p) The prefix to a unit indicating a submultiple of one million-million, *e.g.* 1×10^{-12} of a second is a picosecond.

pictogram A chart that uses symbols instead of figures to represent quantitative data.

pictograph See *pictogram.*

picture Prestel The development of Prestel facilities to allow the insertion of a still picture of color television quality into an information page.

picture processing The analysis, generally by digital signal processing techniques, of the information contained in pictures or images. The original picture may be a drawing, photograph, etc., that is digitized in such a way that it can be regarded as a two dimensional array of data. Each element of the two dimensional array is called a picture element *(pixel).*

PID See *personal identification device.*

pie chart A quantitative representation of data whereby a circle represents the whole amount, *e.g.* total annual sales, and the divisions are proportional slices of the circle (pie).

PILOT A computer programming language specifically designed for creating *computer aided learning* packages. It has fourteen simple commands allowing the author to create sets of questions with routing for the student, depending on the answers given.

pilot operation After the final testing of a new system, changeover from old to new system may be achieved by pilot operation. This may be by retrospective parallel running or staged changeover. Retrospective parallel running is a procedure wherein the new system is run using input data from a previous period, so that the results are known and can be checked. It does not simulate day to day running since it is not so time critical, but it does use less resources than *parallel running.* A staged changeover, sometimes called phased changeover or restricted data running, is a method in which the new system is introduced in piecemeal fashion, by phasing in different areas of the work gradually.

PIN See *personal identification number.*

pin feed printer A printer that has *sprockets* on either end of a *platen* to engage the holes of *continuous form paper.*

PIO Parallel input/output. See *parallel data transmission.*

PIP Peripheral interchange program. A multipurpose and extremely versatile command within the industry standard operating system.

PIPO See *parallel input, parallel output.*

PISO See *parallel input, serial output.*

pitch A measure of character spacing, *e.g.* the number of characters that are printed in a horizontal inch.

pixel An abbreviation for picture element, it is the smallest element in a picture display. See also *picture processing.*

PL/1 A high level programming language developed by the IBM Corporation, to combine the problem solving facilities of *FORTRAN* with the data handling capabilities of *COBOL.*

PLA Programmable logic array. An array of logic elements that can be programmed to perform a specific function.

PLAN A low level language, close to machine code.

platen The rubber-covered cylinder within a printer or typewriter, around which the paper is passed during printing.

PLATO A *computer based learning* system.

platter The *videodisc* used for *IVI.*

PL/M Programming language for microprocessors. See *programming language.*

plotter An output device for translating information into pictorial or graphical form on paper or a similar medium. See also *drum plotter* and *x-y plotter.*

plugboard See *patchboard.*

PMBX See *private manual branch exchange.*

point of sale terminal (POS) A specialized cash register, credit card recording system or ticket dispenser that causes all information concerning the transaction to be relayed to a central computer.

pointer (1) A storage location or register that contains a memory address referring to a specific location in memory. (2) An item of information indicating the address of another item of information.

poke An instruction to modify the contents of an absolute memory location from a high level language, usually by means of a procedure whose two arguments are the address in question and the value to be inserted there. Compare *peek.*

POL See *problem oriented language.*

polarity The positive or negative state of a material capable of being magnetized.

port The point at which signals from terminal equipment enter the central computing system. Generally the port can be switched to input or output and is often associated with a *peripheral interface adapter.*

portability A term used to describe the suitability of a piece of hardware or software for connection or transfer to another machine. Although a piece of software may be readily transferred to another computer, *i.e.* portable, it is not necessarily machine independent.

portable Pertaining to the degree to which a program may be run on machine code programs.

portable computer A computer that is compact, usually comprising keyboard, processor, disk/cassette storage and screen with a single power cable, within a single unit or carrying case.

portable program A program that may be readily transferred to another computer system with a minimum of work.

POS See *point of sale terminal.*

positive presentation Screen display that has black characters on a white background.

postmortem Analysis of the cause of some undesired system behavior, based upon information recorded at the time the error or fault occurred, *e.g. abnormal termination* might provide a *memory dump* as a record of the state of the program at the time of the termination. The memory dump would be used for the postmortem analysis.

postprocessor A program that performs some operations on the output of another program, typically converting output into another form suitable for a different process.

power supply A circuit for converting an a.c. voltage to d.c. in such a way that the output is regulated to minimize noise and voltage fluctuations.

precedence See *operator precedence.*

precompiled code Program code that has already been passed through a *compiler* to produce *relocatable code* that is ready for execution.

preprinted forms Collated multiforms printed with general information, *e.g.* headings and box layout. The computer printer is lined up with the forms and then individual details are printed (variable information).

preprocessor A program that performs modifications to data in order that the data conforms to the input requirements of a standard program, such as a compiler or statistical package.

pre-recorded Having to do with information that was input and stored previously.

preventive maintenance Maintenance performed on a regular basis, and intended to prevent failures, *e.g.* cleaning and lubricating moving parts and checking the performance and tolerance of circuits.

primary document The source document from which all processing originates.

primary storage Another name for primary memory, *main store* or main memory.

print queue A list of printing jobs that have to be done in one certain order. See also *queue.*

print styles The various combinations of print *typeface* and *pitch* of printing.

printed circuit An electronic circuit design in which the connections between the terminals of individual components are formed from copper conductors laminated onto a flat supporting sheet of an insulating material such as fiberglass. Components are usually placed on the reverse side of the board with their terminals through holes for connection by hand or dip soldering to the copper circuits. The supporting sheet plus the circuit is known as the printed circuit board.

printed circuit board (PCB) See *printed circuit.*

printer An output device producing characters or graphic symbols on paper. See also *band, barrel, daisy wheel, dot matrix, ink jet, laser, line, page, thermal* and *xerographic printers.*

printer control characters Characters or character combinations that are included in computer output in order to transfer suitable control commands to the printer, *e.g.* new line, overprinting, reduced print, etc.

printer ribbon The ribbon used by *impact printers.*

printout Output from a computer controlled printer.

printwheel A removable printing element in the shape of a flat wheel with many spokes, each with a character at its tip. Printwheels come in various type sizes and styles.

priority The active status given a program in a *multiprogramming system.* The priority of a program determines how much CPU time (how many time slices) it will get.

priority scheduling A method of task dispatching based on a priority scheme. Each program is given a priority and is executed on the basis of what other programs have higher priority.

privacy of data The protection against unauthorized retrieval of data.

privacy of information One aspect concerns the protection of data owned by an individual or corporate entity such that security processes are used to restrict unauthorized access. The second concept concerns the right of an individual or corporate entity to be informed that information concerning them is held within a computer system and to uphold their right to view the information if requested. See also *data protection legislation.*

privacy transformation The use of *encryption* methods to encode, store and decode sensitive information.

private automatic branch exchange (PABX) A telephone system that enables extension users to dial their own external calls without going through the switchboard; extensions can dial one another. Calls coming in from the outside must be dealt with by the switchboard operator.

private automatic exchange (PAX) This is entirely separate from the public exchange system, but allows users to contact one another quickly.

private data network A data network privately owned by a company or organization. Access is limited and therefore greater security of data is possible, but any network over long distances will be expensive to set up, hence the growth of *value added networks.*

private manual branch exchange (PMBX) An internal telephone system where all outgoing and incoming calls, and all calls made between extensions, have to go through the switchboard.

.PRL An *extension* that indicates a page-relocatable file (like a .COM file) that can be executed in the MP/M operating system. The file may be relocated to any page boundary, a necessity when the system has multiple partitions.

problem oriented language (POL) A programming language whose control structures and data structures reflect in some measure the characteristics of a class of problems, *e.g.* business data processing and scientific computation applications require languages with different types of facilities.

procedure A section of a program that is identified by name and that carries out some well defined operations on data. Data items and information to control the procedure process are passed by means of parameters that can change whenever the procedure is called. The term procedure is generally used in the context of *high level programming languages* whereas the term subroutine is more commonly used in conjunction with *assembly language* routines. See also *subprogram.*

process control The use of a dedicated computer to control a specific industrial or manufacturing process. Information from the process, *e.g.* temperature and pressure, is used as a source of data that is analyzed and results in control signals, *e.g.* to adjust a pressure valve, being sent back to the process. See also *numerical control, computer aided/assisted manufacturing.*

process descriptor In the MP/M operating system, the process descriptor keeps track of all parameters of a task or process.

processing A systematic sequence of operations to produce a desired result.

processor A computer, usually the *central processor* component.

professional workstations High quality terminals offering word processing, graphics, extensive calculator functions and information retrieval.

program (1) A set of statements that can be submitted as a unit to some computer system and used to direct the behavior of the system. (2) The start-up of the system and the loading of a software program.

program counter A counting *register* that normally increments one memory *address* at a time and is used to obtain the program sequence from sequential memory locations.

program cross-reference list A list of program components and references that enables a programmer to check the location and use of specific constructions in the code.

program design language (PDL) A language used for expressing program designs. They are similar to a high level programming language but emphasize structure and intention rather than detail for program execution. PDLs are often employed in conjunction with *structured programming,* and when the content is not executable, they are termed *pseudocode.*

program development system A computer system that provides support to the program development phase of a software project. A typical system will include data base or filing facilities for storing information and project documentation; and software for editing program source text, compiling, link loading and debugging. Compare *software engineering environment.*

program disk A disk which contains both the *operating system* and the *applications* software.

program execution When a computer carries out the instructions specified by a computer program.

program generator A program that assists users to write their own programs, by expanding simple statements into program code.

program instruction An *instruction* within a program.

program language See *programming language.*

program library A collection of programs and packages that are available for use. Some items might be independent software that is processed with user data; others could be routines that are incorporated automatically, when referenced in other programs.

program listing An output list of program source code. At the end of the compilation process, a compiler can produce a program listing with error diagnostics.

program maintenance All technical activities associated with a particular program once it has been formally released for operational use. This may include extensions and modifications as well as the correction of errors.

program specification A precise statement of the effects that an individual program is required to achieve. It is not required to state how a result will be achieved.

program statement A *source language* instruction that generates several *machine code* instructions when translated by a *compiler.*

program structure The overall form of a program that emphasizes the individual components and their interrelationships. A well structured program will have logical units of code (having a single entry point and single exit point) with clear, simple links to other components within a program. A poorly structured program may have few or no identifiable components with complex code sequences. See also *structured programming.*

program testing Executing a program with data that will provide known results for checking.

program verification All forms of checking and testing that will ensure that the program will do exactly what it is supposed to do.

programmable calculator A *calculator* that has a capacity to retain stored instructions for repetitive calculations.

programmable device A device that will obey a sequence of stored instructions.

programmable read only memory (PROM) This is similar to a *ROM* chip whose *nonvolatile memory* is used to store a fixed program. However, it can be programmed for permanent use in a particular application. Compare *erasable programmable read only memory.*

programmed correspondence The ability of word processing systems to store text for subsequent inclusion in a document.

programmed learning Software that enables an individual to carry out a course of self study controlled by the computer. See also *computer aided/assisted instruction, computer aided/assisted learning, computer based learning,* and *computer managed learning.*

programmer A person responsible for writing computer programs.

programming The action of writing and developing programs.

programming in logic (PROLOG) See *PROLOG.*

programming language An artificial language constructed in such a way that people and programmable machines can communicate with each other in a precise manner. They do not permit the freedom of expression that is found in *natural languages.*

programming standards A set of rules or conventions that constrain the form in which programs are produced within an organization.

programming support environment See *software engineering environment.*

PROLOG Programming in logic. A programming language based on mathematical logic, with applications in information retrieval and artificial intelligence systems.

PROM See *programmable read only memory.*

prompt A cue or message issued by a processing system that guides the user during interactive applications.

proof A hard copy of a document to be marked for errors and revisions.

proportional spacing A method of printing in which each character printed takes up only the space it needs, rather than a fixed amount of space as in *monospacing, e.g.* the letter i needs less space than the letter m.

protected field A portion of data that cannot be modified directly by the operator.

protection See *data protection legislation.*

protocol Any agreement that governs the procedures used to exchange information between cooperating entities. In general a protocol will include: the definition of message formats, the sequencing rules concerning messages and the interpretation rules concerning messages transferred in proper sequence.

prototyping system A hardware system used to *breadboard* a microprocessor-based product.

pseudo digital The modulated analog signals (produced by a *modem)* carrying digital information on the public switched telephone network.

pseudo random numbers A sequence of *random numbers* that are generated from a specific start point and which can be reproduced if necessary.

pseudocode An informal notation, similar to program code, which is used to describe functions within a *procedure* or program. See also *program design language.*

PSS Packet Switch Stream. See *packet switching.*

p-type material A type of semiconductor that has been made more positive by the addition of an impurity such as phosphorous which reduces the number of available electrons. See also *n-type material.*

pulse width modulation A method of voltage regulation, for switching power supplies, in which energy delivered to the d.c. output is controlled by varying the conduction or 'on' time of the switching devices.

punch paper tape See *paper tape.*

punched card A thin card that may have a series of holes punched in its vertical columns to hold encoded data ready for transfer to the computer. The most common card has 80 columns with 12 rows of punch positions in each column. Each character corresponds to a specific combination of vertical holes so one card may hold up to 80 individual numbers or characters. The last type of card to be widely used was a 96 column IBM card.

punched card reader An input device that senses data encoded on a card as a pattern of holes and converts it into a series of binary codes for the computer.

punched tag A small card that is encoded with a pattern of holes and attached to a product in a shop or factory. When the product is sold or transferred, the tag or part of it is removed and read as part of a data capture process, *e.g. Kimball tag* in retail applications.

purging Erasing or deleting unnecessary files from the system.

push button dialing Defining the destination code for a telephone call by pressing numbered buttons compared with the older system of using a rotary dial. A rotary dial 'makes and breaks' the subscriber's telephone link to define a required number, the push button system sends a voice frequency tone for each number.

Q

QBE See *query by example.*

QL See *query language.*

Qube A *videotex* system.

quad density disk drive A *drive* that stores information on both surfaces of a disk.

query by example (QBE) A way of retrieving information by specifying the items required in appropriate positions of a standard format displayed on a *VDU* screen.

query language The section of a *data base management system* that provides facilities for the interrogation of the data base. A language designed to access a data base directly from a terminal is known as an interactive query language.

query processing The processing of a transaction against a file or database, such that information is abstracted but the data contents remain unchanged. The term can also apply to the translation of a series of query commands, in a query language, into executable commands.

queue A list where all insertions are made at one end of the list and the removals and accesses are made at the other. Also referred to as a *first in-first out* list (FIFO), pushup stack or pushup list. Queues are frequently used to buffer input and output processes, *e.g.* a print queue holds a list of references for files waiting to be printed.

queue management The queue manager software controls the activities whereby an item may be added to a *queue,* then subsequently selected for processing.

quicksort A form of sorting by exchanging records developed by C. A. Hoare that compares *sortkeys* from the two extremes of the file alternately working up the file from the bottom until an exchange is necessary and then working down the file from the top.

QWERTY The typewriter key layout that is most frequently used for computer keyboards.

R

radio paging service A service that allows the wearer of a radio receiving device to be contacted by dialing a particular telephone number. The device 'beeps' to alert the person that someone wishes to make contact, *e.g.* used by hospital doctors, business sales and service personnel, etc.

radio spectrum See *frequency.*

radio telephone See *radiophone.*

radio transmission The transmission of data by means of radio signals.

radiophone A telephone that is not connected by wires to a telephone communication system but communicates via radio transmissions. There is a limited bandwidth available for radiophone transmissions so the numbers of subscribers and the quality of the service is limited. However, new developments provide improved facilities via *cellular radio* services.

ragged right See *ragged text.*

ragged text Text that is not presented as a column, *i.e.* the right hand side of the text is not straight. See also *unjustified text* and *justification.*

RAM See *random access memory.*

random access A type of memory access for which the access time to any item is independent of the address of that item and independent of the address of the previous item. The term can be applied to *main memory* or *backing store* devices such as magnetic drum or disk. Media such as magnetic tape are not random access devices.

random access file A file held on a *random access* device, such that individual records, or parts of records, may be accessed without reading the rest of the file.

random access memory (RAM) The term tends to be associated with semiconductor memory which is equivalent to *core store,* but magnetic memories can equally be called RAM.

random allocation A software function whereby *sectors* are randomly allocated to files as needed, as opposed to *sequential allocation.*

random numbers Numbers that are obtained using a sampling technique to obtain a series of values from a set of permissible numbers. True random numbers, which cannot be reproduced for checking and debugging purposes, are difficult to obtain.

raster graphics See *raster mode graphics display.*

raster mode graphics display A method of presenting graphical or pictorial images in which the desired shape is built up by means of a succession of parallel movements of the pen or a plotter or the spot on a VDU. The technique is similar to that which generates a television picture.

raster scan A mode of exploration or reproduction of an image by tracing a series of adjacent parallel lines. See also *raster mode graphics display.*

rational number A number that can be expressed as a ratio of two integer numbers. The first integer is the numerator, the second is the denominator, *e.g.* 6/5.

raw data The data as entered into the computer, before any *validation* or processing.

reactance The component of the *impedance* of an a.c. circuit which is due to *inductance* or *capacitance* in the circuit.

read head See *read/write head.*

read only memory (ROM) A *nonvolatile semiconductor memory* device that holds data or instructions permanently. The device is programmed during manufacture and cannot be altered by the computer or programmer.

read/write head A magnetic head that can read, write and erase data encoded on *magnetic media.*

ready to receive A *signal* sent by a receiving unit upon receipt of a *request to send* signal.

real-time clock A clock that runs regardless of whether processes that refer to the clock are running or not. A real-time clock measures elapsed time. Compare *relative-time clock.*

real-time processing Processing carried out by a *real-time system.*

real-time system Any system that is able to receive continuously changing data from outside sources and which is able to process the data sufficiently rapidly to be capable of influencing the sources of data, *e.g.* process control, air traffic control, airline bookings.

real number Any number with a fractional part, *e.g.* 1.25. In *FORTRAN* and some other *high level programming languages,* 'real' is used to indicate *floating point* storage.

real time The time elapsed between events occurring externally to the microcomputer.

recall A term used in information processing to mean retrieval or file transfer from *backing store, e.g.* recall a document file for editing.

recognition logic The software in an optical character reader that enables the scanner to translate printed text into digital information.

record A collection of data relating to one subject. Each record may consist of several *fields* of information.

records management A feature of some word processing systems whereby the word processor can be used to create, edit, store, sort and select, and print information that is not necessarily related to text *e.g.* maintaining lists of customers and their details. See also *file management* and *data base management.*

recovery The process of restoring normal operation after the occurrence of a fault.

recursion The situation when a specific function or procedure requires a call to itself to carry out its required purpose.

redundancy The provision of additional components in a system, over and above the minimum set required to perform the functions of the system, for purposes of *reliability* or *robustness.*

reference file A file that will remain relatively unchanged over a long period of time, so that other files can refer to records in it.

reformat To change the *format* of text, involving changes to *margins, page lengths, pitch, justification,* etc.

refresh To repeat, at regular intervals, the display of digital information on a *VDU* or television *monitor,* in order that the display can appear continuous.

regenerate See *refresh.*

register A special type of store location in a computer, used for a specific purpose, *e.g.* store register, instruction register, accumulator register.

register pair On the 8080 or Z80, a pair of registers such as HL, BC, DE may be treated as one 16-bit register instead of two 8-bit registers for certain operations.

regulation The percentage change in output voltage when the load goes from full load to no load.

regulation-line A power supply's ability to eliminate, within a specified range, the output voltage deviations as the result of input line changes.

regulation-load A power supply's ability to eliminate, within a specified range, the output voltage deviations as the result of load magnitude changes.

rehyphenation The process of inserting or deleting *hyphens* in text where the line length has changed as a result of changed *margin* settings.

relational data base A form of data base specification based upon the mathematical concept of a relation. The data base structure may be regarded as a set of rectangular tables, each expressing one relation. Compared to a network or *hierarchical data base,* the structure and links between items are set up every time a query is made.

relational operator See *logical operator.*

relative-time clock A free running clock that raises an *interrupt* at regular intervals. These interrupts allow the supervisory program to track the passage of real time. See also *real-time clock.*

reliability The ability of a computer system to perform its required functions for a given period of time. Reliability is often quoted as a percentage of *uptime* but may be more usefully expressed as *mean time between failures.*

relocatable code Code that can be moved anywhere in memory since it does not contain any absolute memory *addresses.*

remedial maintenance Sometimes known as corrective maintenance, this work takes place after a fault is found in order to correct that fault. Compare *preventive maintenance.*

remote A term used to describe a process, system or piece of equipment that uses a communication link to reach the computer, *e.g. remote job entry,* remote terminal.

remote control The control of a device via a remote communicator, handset or terminal. The term is usually associated with controls that use radio communication methods.

remote device Any device that has the required communication *interface* enabling it to be used remotely.

remote job entry (RJE) A system by which a communications link is used to submit work from an input device and to receive results on a printer or other output medium.

remote terminal A terminal that is some distance from the computer and requires a communication link. If the transmission is over the *PSTN* then a *modem* will be required to convert the digital data signals to analog signals for transmission.

rename To change the name or some other identifier of a document or file held on *backing store, e.g.* disk file name.

repagination The process of changing the lengths of pages, which may be required if text has been inserted or deleted from a document. Repagination involves the automatic or manual repositioning of *page breaks* in text.

repeat key A word processing function that allows a character to be repeated many times without continually rekeying it.

report generator (RPG) A programming language used in commercial data processing for extracting information from files. The input consists of a file structure description followed by a specification of the information required and how it should be presented. From this information the RPG constructs a program to read the file, extract the information and format the output in the required manner. The best known example of an RPG is RPG II.

reprographics The field of automatically reproducing documents through a variety of techniques.

request to send A signal sent by a transmitting unit indicating that it is ready to send data.

required hyphen A hyphen that occurs normally in a word regardless of its position in a piece of text, *e.g.* user-friendly. A required hyphen is not removed automatically by the system during *rehyphenation.*

required space A word processing facility which ensures that groups of closely related words such as names and dates are not placed on two separate lines by the word wraparound feature.

rerun To run a program or transmission process again, usually after a machine malfunction.

rescue dump A copy of the workspace associated with a process, taken with a view to allowing the process to be restarted following a system failure. See also *dump.*

reserved word An identifier or name that has a specific meaning within a programming language and therefore is not available for use by the programmer. See also *keyword.*

reset/clear To set a *register* or counter to the all-zero state. Also used in conjunction with clearing a display screen.

resident Permanently present in *main memory,* as compared with information that is temporary and loaded from *backing store* as necessary.

resident console commands Commands that are built into the console command interpreter which must be loaded from disk to be executed. Generally, the only commands made resident are the most frequently used (and least destructive) of the system-level commands.

resident software Assembler and editor programs incorporated with a prototyping system to aid in user program writing and development.

resistance The property of a substance by virtue of which it resists the flow of an electric *current* through it. See also *resistor.*

resistor A device or material that limits the flow of *current* when a *voltage* is applied.

resistor transistor logic (RTL) An early logic family, usually produced in *integrated circuit* form. Despite its low power dissipation, RTL is now little used since it has relatively slow switching speed and small *fan-out.*

resolution The amount of graphical information that can be shown on a visual display. The resolution is usually quantified by the number of lines that can be distinguished visually. The resolution of a computer graphics system is also defined by the number of points or *pixels* that may be displayed in the vertical and horizontal directions. See also *high resolution graphics* and *low resolution graphics.*

response time The elapsed time between an action by a computer system user and the receipt of some sort of response or feedback from the system.

restore To reset to an earlier value, *e.g.* when a process is about to be *rerun,* the initial contents of files are reset to their original state from *back-up* copies.

restricted data running See *pilot operation.*

reticle An *integrated circuit* pattern that contains the design of an integrated circuit *chip.* The reticle is initially some 500 times larger than the final chip layout, as it needs to be checked manually before it is transferred to a photographic plate. Further checks are made and errors corrected before the reticle pattern is finally reduced to the actual size of the chip.

retrieval The recall of a file to the screen.

retrospective parallel running See *pilot operation.*

return A process whereby a *subprogram,* upon completion of its processing, turns control of the processor back to the program (or subprogram) that invoked it.

reverse field characters Those characters on a screen display which are presented for emphasis in the opposite color combination from the majority of the screen, *e.g.* if the majority of text is white letters on a black background, highlighted characters would be displayed as black on small white squares.

reverse video Highlighting parts of a screen by reversing the normal foreground and background colors. See also *reverse field characters.*

RF See *frequency.*

rig counter A loop formed of interconnected bistable devices for counting a sequence in input signals.

right justification Data fields which contain information such that the rightmost characters/bits within a field are filled first and any spaces are to the left of the field. See also *justification.*

rigid disks Hard *magnetic disks.*

ring data network A network constructed as a loop of unidirectional links between *stations.* Data received on an incoming link will either be copied into the station's memory (if the recipient) or passed onto the outgoing link for transfer to the next station in the loop. See also *star network* and *bus network.*

ripple The a.c. voltage on the output of the power supply related to the input source and/or to the internal switching frequencies. Normally ripple is specified as a peak to peak amplitude with a frequency range.

RJE See *remote job entry.*

RMS See *root mean square.*

RMS line current The square root of the average of the squares of all the instantaneous current amplitudes occurring during one cycle.

robot A programmable device consisting of mechanical manipulators and sensory organs that are linked to a computer. Most robots in current industrial use are programmed to repeat a routine sequence of instructions.

robotics A discipline concerned with *artificial intelligence,* electronics and mechanical engineering. It is concerned with building *robots.*

robustness A measure of the ability of a system to recover from error conditions, whether generated internally or externally.

rogue value See *terminator.*

roll in/roll out A method of handling memory in a system dealing with a number of simultaneously active processes. When a program and/or data is read into memory from a disk it is called roll-in. Roll-out is when it is no longer required in memory or its processing *time slice* is complete and it is transferred back to disk.

rollback (software) The action of obtaining a software reload after the original has become corrupt.

ROM See *read only memory.*

romware Software stored permanently in a *ROM, PROM, EPROM, EEROM, EAROM* or *EAPROM.*

root mean square (RMS) For example, r.m.s. line current is the square root of the average of the squares of all the instantaneous current *amplitudes* occurring during one cycle.

ROS Read only storage. Storage into which data cannot be written during program execution and thus containing nonalterable data and instructions.

round robin A method of allocating *central processor* time in a multiuser environment. Each user is allocated a portion of time and when it has been used control passes to the next user.

round-robin system In time sharing, a processing technique whereby each user is serviced for a predetermined period of time.

rounding The process of approximating a number by its nearest equivalent, to a set number of significant figures, *e.g.* the value 2.346 would be rounded up to 2.35 if accuracy to two decimal places is required. See also *truncation.*

RPG See *report program generator.*

RPG II One of the earliest examples of a *report generator* language.

RS-232C An input/output *port* standard common to many *microcomputers.*

RTL See *resistor transistor logic.*

ruler (format line) In some word processing software, a line on the screen which gives information about the format of the document being worked on; *e.g.,* margins and tabs.

run What a program does when it is performing.

run time error An error detected during *program execution.*

running foot The line of copy that appears at the bottom of a page.

S

S-100 (standard bus) See *bus.*

satellite A man-made device that has been launched on a rocket into space and that orbits earth. A geostationary satellite goes around the globe once every 24 hours so appears stationary over one point of the earth's surface. These types of satellites are equipped with signal receiving and transmitting equipment usually powered by energy from solar cells. Thus signals can be received by the satellite from a range of ground stations and transmitted down to another part of the earth's surface.

satellite broadcasting Early telecommunications *satellites* had very little power and signal *broadcasting* required large diameter dishes for transmitting and receiving *aerials.* With improvements in technology, it is now possible for satellites to output more power into the transmitted signals and to focus the transmission to a small part of the earth's surface. See also *direct broadcasting by satellite.*

satellite computer A computer that forms part of a computing system but is generally much less capable than the *mainframe computer.* It is often located at a distance from the main system and provides auxiliary functions as *remote* data entry. With the development of *microcomputer* based terminals, the term has become synonymous with terminal.

satellite network A series of *satellites* orbiting the earth, operated by a single organization such as *INTELSAT* to provide communication links across the world via satellite transmissions.

scale factor A multiplier used to scale one or more quantities so they fall within a prescribed range of values.

scaling The adjustment of values to be used in a computation so that they and their resultant are within the range that can be handled by a process or piece of equipment. This is achieved by applying a scaling factor and often the values are readjusted before a result is output.

scanner device Any device such as a *bar code reader* or *optical character recognition* equipment that travels over predefined lines, shapes or characters and *decodes* them into *digital signals* which a computer can interpret.

scheduler The program or code responsible for controlling the use of shared resources such as *CPU, printers* and *storage devices.*

scheduling The action carried out by a scheduler, e.g. the CPU scheduler is the method by which *CPU* time is allotted in a *multiaccess system.* This may be as simple as *round robin* or as complex as a scheme of priorities distinguishing between users and tasks.

schema The formal description of the data structure in a database. A complex database system will have a number of schemata corresponding to various user descriptions, the conceptual logical description and the physical description.

scientific calculator A *calculator* provided with special mathematical and scientific functions to work out complex scientific or engineering formulas. Some scientific calculators have *keyboards* specifically designed for a specialist application, e.g. statistics. See also *programmable calculator.*

scratch file See *work file.*

scratch tape A magnetic tape used for *scratch files.*

scratchpad A type of semiconductor memory that usually has a small capacity but very fast access. It is used for temporary storage of intermediate results and may also be called *working store.*

screen (1) The video device on which text and data are displayed at a *VDU.* (2) The amount of text and data that can fit on the screen. (3) What is displayed on the screen, including the graphic elements and layout.

screen buffer A *buffer* used to store the data that is displayed on the screen of a *VDU.*

screen dump An activity that reproduces the contents of a visual display screen on paper media, e.g. *printer* or *plotter.*

screen editor See *text editor.*

scroll To move the information displayed on a *screen* to the top or bottom of a display area. As information disappears at one edge, new information becomes visible at the other. The scrolling action appears as a smooth movement.

SDLC See *synchronous data link control.*

SDT (system device table) A collection of data for keeping track of all devices available to the system.

search and replace A word processing function that searches a document for a specific string of characters and replaces it with another character string.

search key A *key* (sense 2) defined by a file user for the computer process to check with record values when carrying out a search or retrieval.

second generation computers Computers whose designs were started after 1955, constructed with both vacuum tube *(valve)* technology and discrete *transistor* logic, providing internal operating speeds in the order of microseconds, using a wider range of input/output media including high performance magnetic tape and early forms of on-line storage such as *magnetic drums* and *ferrite core* memory. The hardware became smaller and more reliable but was still relatively expensive although the available processing power was now being scheduled via the introduction of *time sharing* and *real-time system* applications. See also *first, third, fourth* and *fifth generation computers.*

secondary extents The space allowed to *disk files* when the first *directory* entry becomes full.

secondary storage (auxiliary storage, external storage) Storage in addition to the computer's *random access memory.*

sector A portion of a rotational magnetic storage device that can be accessed by the magnetic head in the course of a particular rotation.

sector allocation A software function whereby sectors are kept track of in a sector pool and are allocated as needed to files on a disk.

sector mapping A method of improving disk *access time* by skewing or shifting sector addresses around the disk.

security checks Public and private computer systems usually require each user to identify themselves by a code number and/or *password* before access is granted. See also *security of data and files.*

security of data and files Protection against unauthorized alteration of stored *data. Files* may be stored such that access and/or update privileges are applicable to

(a) only the owner of the file, (b) a selected group of other users or (c) all other users.

seek time The time taken for a particular track on a storage disk or drum to be located. Typical times are in the range 10 to 30 milliseconds.

select code A number assigned to *I/O channels* for identification in information transfers between the microcomputer and external devices.

self-checking numbers Codes or numbers that include a *check digit* to assist with data *validation.*

semantics That part of a language that defines the meaning associated with individual words, phrases or symbols.

semaphore A special purpose data type. It may be used in two types of operations, *i.e. wait* and *signal.* A wait operation decreases the integer semaphore by one, providing it does not go negative, and the signal operation increases it by one. Thus a wait operation on a semaphore value of one indicates that a free resource is about to be used and any subsequent wait operation will continue to wait until the semaphore value is above zero again.

semiconductor A material such as *silicon* or *germanium,* whose electrical conductivity increases with temperature and is intermediate between metals and *insulators.* Semiconductors of different conductivity can be combined to provide a variety of junctions that are the basis of semiconductor devices such as *transistors.* See also *bipolar transistor, field effect transistor* and *junction transistor.*

sentinel A data item that indicates the value of some important state, *e.g.* an *end of data* sentinel means all the data has been read. See also *terminator* and *flag.*

sequential access The location of a stored *file* by searching through the files, one after another until the desired file is reached.

sequential allocation A software function whereby *sectors* are sequentially allocated to *disk files,* rather than randomly allocated.

sequential file A file with records stored in a logical sequence according to the value of a *key field* (by sequence) or a file with records stored in the order in which they are created (entry sequence).

serial access A method of data access in which blocks of data are read from the storage medium in the physical order in which they occur, until the required item is reached.

serial character Pertaining to a *printer* that prints one character at a time.

serial data transmission Transmission where the bits are sent one by one along the same data line. Compare *parallel data transmission.*

serial file See *sequential file.*

serial input/output (SIO) A method of transferring data between devices, typically a computer and its peripherals. The individual data bits are sent sequentially. Compare *parallel data transmission* and see also *serial data transmission.*

serial input, parallel output (SIPO) A term used to describe devices that can accept several serial data streams and convert them to a single parallel data stream. Compare *parallel input, serial output.*

serial input, serial output (SISO) A term used to describe devices where information can only enter or leave via *serial data transmission* methods.

serial interface A *peripheral* interface to the *central processing unit* by way of the *system bus* that sends and receives data serially from another computer or terminal.

serial printer A printer that prints one character at a time in the sequence in which they appear in a line of text. It is less efficient than a *line printer* for large quantities of output with long lines, but it is more practical for documents with short lines or preprinted forms requiring a minimum of output.

set A data structure consisting of zero or more elements of a given data type. Sets can grow or shrink dynamically, but each element must have a unique value.

shadow ROM A term used to describe *read only memory* that may be switched out of memory space after its contents (operating system) have been loaded into the microcomputer's *random access memory*.

shared facility Any facility such as a *printer* or *disk storage* device that can be assigned temporarily to an individual *workstation* within a system.

shared logic system A system in which several terminals share a *CPU* simultaneously. This usually means that the terminals can communicate with each other and *peripheral* devices via a *network*.

shared logic text processor A *text processing* facility using a *shared logic system*.

shared resources system A system whereby *stand-alone* workstations can share expensive resources such as *printers* and *disk storage*. The *workstations* are still independent of each other and can only communicate with the shared peripherals, not with each other.

sheet feeder A device that can be attached to a *word processor* that feeds single sheets of paper.

shellsort A sorting *algorithm* that is a variant of a *straight insertion sort,* it allows records to take long leaps rather than move one position at a time.

SHF See *super high frequency.*

shift key A key that enables one *character set* to be interpreted as another set, *e.g.* normal typewriter use where a key produces a lowercase letter unless the shift key is depressed.

short circuit protection A current-limiting system that enables a power supply to continue operating without damage in any output overload including short circuits. The output voltage must be restored to normal when the overload is removed, as distinguished from a fuse or circuit breaker system that opens at overload and must be reclosed to restore power.

sign off See *logging off.*

sign on See *logging on.*

signal A form of data that is usually envisaged as a sequence of values, *e.g.* a continuously changing quantity such as *amplitude* plotted against time, or a series of discrete *digital* codes.

signal code The series of pulses that creates 1 byte of information.

signal processing The processing of *signals* by means of *hardwired* or *programmable devices.* The signals may be continuous or discrete being approximated by analog or digital devices accordingly, *e.g. picture processing.* See also *digital signal processing.*

silicon An inexpensive and widely available semiconductor material that has replaced *germanium* in most electronic *solid state devices.* Although it is the second most abundant chemical element, it does not occur naturally and must be obtained from the natural forms of silicon dioxide (sand and quartz).

silicon chip A *chip* based on the element *silicon.*

silicon on sapphire (SOS) A metal-oxide semiconductor technology in which a layer of single crystal silicon is grown onto a synthetic sapphire substrate. Since the sapphire substrate is insulating, lower *capacitances* are achieved that improve the switching speeds and packing densities of the devices. However, the substrate material is more expensive to produce than silicon.

silicon wafer A *wafer* based on *silicon.*

simplex operation A transmission system that allows transmission to take place in one direction only.

SIMULA A programming language based on *ALGOL* 60 with extensions to make it suitable for writing *simulation* programs.

simulation Imitation of the behavior of some existing or intended system. By experimenting on a model, whether physical or mathematical, valuable insight is gained into the likely behavior of the real system. It is a particularly useful technique when the real item under investigation is too expensive to build, too dangerous to experiment with or requires a long time scale to 'see' the effect of changing system or model parameters. Computer simulation programs are widely used in industry and commerce, *e.g.* pilot training simulators, weather forecasting, traffic flow, economic forecasts, chemical plant models.

simulator A program that simulates the actions of the *central processor,* allowing a program to be stepped through, instruction by instruction, to determine where errors are occurring.

sine wave A wave that can be expressed as the sine of a linear function of time, space or both.

single density A term used to denote that storage of information within a medium such as a *disk* is not compressed in any way.

single-feed sheet A *printer* attachment that automatically feeds one individual sheet of paper into the printer in response to a signal from the printer.

single line display A display screen that allows a single line of information to be presented at a time. These small screens are frequently found on *electronic typewriters,* small portable computers and *calculators.*

single strike ribbon A type of *carbon ribbon* that is only good for one pass of the printer, after which it is discarded. It gives the highest quality ribbon print.

single user system A system that permits single user operation only, *e.g. stand-alone systems* of *microcomputers.*

SIO See *serial input/output.*

SIPO See *serial input, parallel output.*

SISO See *serial input, serial output.*

sixteen bit Pertaining to microprocessors that operate with a 16-bit word.

skip An instruction that causes the microprocessor to omit the instruction in the immediately following location.

slave A computer with enough memory to run an operating system that is tied into a distributed network.

slave processor A computer, which may or may not be as powerful or as fast as the master or system processor;

it is used to perform simple but time-consuming tasks for the master, freeing the master to do other things.

small scale integration (SSI) About 10 components on a single *integrated circuit.*

smart card A plastic card similar to a *credit card* but having some memory and a microprocessor embedded within it. It can store and calculate details of transactions for which it is being used. Although originally developed as a form of *electronic money*, it is also useful for identification and access control passes, holding personal data such as medical information, etc. Its high technology component is thought to minimize fraud and forgery.

smart terminal See *intelligent terminal.*

snaking columns Side-by-side columns (newspaper style) in which the second and subsequent columns are a continuation of the previous column.

SNOBOL A programming language for the manipulation of character *strings.* It incorporates powerful pattern matching and string searching operations.

Society for Worldwide Financial Telecommunications (SWIFT) An international banking *data network* developed in the late 1970s. By 1983 it linked 900 banks in more than 39 countries.

sociotechnical design A method and approach to systems design that gives as much priority to human organizational and long term aspects as to technical and short term economic requirements.

soft copy A nondurable form of data output, such as text on a screen or output from an audio response unit.

soft hyphen Hyphen input by the system for line-end word division. The system can eliminate the hyphen and reunite the word if room becomes available due to editing.

soft key A key that may have its function changed via software control. See also *soft keyboard.*

soft keyboard A *keyboard* in which the function or code generated by pressing a key can be allocated or changed by program control. Many keyboards have essential functions *hardwired* but also provide soft keys that can be changed with each program application or set at installation time to perform a specific action. See also *function keys.*

soft programmable key A key that can be programmed to perform a series of commands so that when that key is pressed, the commands will be carried out automatically.

soft return A return input by the system during word *wraparound;* it can be altered by the system if required during editing.

soft sector Pertaining to a floppy disk in which one hole, on the disk, is used to synchronize the beginning of the data tracks.

soft sectored disk The size and position of *sectors* on the disk is determined by control electronics and software.

soft zone See *hot zone.*

software A generic term for those components of a computer system that are not physically identifiable. The term is most frequently used to refer to programs and *documentation.* See also *hardware.*

software engineering The discipline of producing reliable software which can be maintained and modified. It is particularly important for large software systems.

software engineering environment A computer system that provides support for the development, repair and enhancement of programs; and for the management and control of these activities. A typical system contains a central database and a set of *software tools*. Compare *program development system.*

software house A company whose primary business is to produce software or assist in the production of software. Software houses may offer a range of services including hiring out suitably qualified staff to join a client's team, consultancy and a complete system design and development service.

software life cycle The complete lifetime of a software product from initial conception to final obsolescence. Typical phases include: system requirements, software requirements, overall design, detailed design, component production, component testing, integration and system testing, release to users, operation and maintenance. Several activities may be repeated as errors are found and corrected and new requirements need to be included.

software maintenance See *program maintenance.*

software packages See *application packages.*

software quality assurance (SQA) The process of ensuring that a software system and its associated documentation are of sufficient quality for their purpose. Often a quality assurance activity will follow the completion of a system development, prior to its release for operational use. This is likely to include functional testing of software, checks on programming standards, ensuring that documentation is complete and suitable for both users and future maintenance requirements.

software reliability A measure of the extent to which a software system can be expected to deliver a service when that service is demanded. Reliability is related to the dynamic demands made upon a system and the ability to produce a satisfactory response. This is usually a function of design and implementation rather than correctness of program code. Compare *robustness.*

software specification A precise statement of the effects that the software component of a system is required to achieve. See also *program specification.*

software system Software to perform a single or related set of tasks.

software tool A program that is employed in the development, repair or enhancement of other programs, *e.g. text editor, compiler,* link loader, debugging tools. Such a set of tools concerned with the program production phase would be provided by a *program development system.* Tools that assist all activities in a *software life cycle* would frequently form part of a *software engineering environment.*

solid font printer Any type of *impact printer* in which the complete shape of each character is engraved or molded onto a font carrier such as a molded ball or wheel *(daisy wheel printer)*, an etched band of metal *(band printer)* or a set of separate type slugs driven around a track *(train printer)*. Compare *matrix printer.*

solid state device A device formed on, or concerned with the circuitry on, a single *chip* of *semiconductor* material, usually *silicon* and therefore comprising *bipolar* or *field effect transistors.*

solid state memory device A device using *semiconductor* memory.

son file See *ancestral file system.*

sort See *sorting.*

sorting The process of rearranging information into an ascending or descending order. An internal sorting method keeps the information within the computer's high speed *random access memory,* an external sorting method uses *backing store.* There are a variety of methods for sorting and the choice of *algorithm* should be made according to the likely characteristics of the data. See also *bubble sort, heapsort, quicksort, shellsort, straight insertion sort, straight selection sort, tree selection sort.*

sortkey The information associated with a record that is to be compared in a *sort* process.

sort/merge program Many data processing files are updated using a sort/merge program. If the initial file is in alphabetical order, then the new records are sorted into alphabetical order. This file is then merged with the initial file to produce a third output file in alphabetical order.

SOS See *silicon on sapphire.*

source code The form of a program that is input to a *compiler, translator* or *interpreter.*

source document A document used for the initial recording of information that will be subsequently processed.

source language The language in which the input to a *compiler, translator* or *interpreter* is written.

source listing A listing of a program in its original *high level language* form.

source program A program written by a user in a high or low level language, *i.e.* in a format prior to translation.

spark printer A printer that provides a *dot matrix* output by means of an electric spark to form the dots by burning them into specially coated paper. As there is no moving type, they can print a line at a time and attain high speeds of operation.

specifications for programs See *program specification.*

speech communication in the office See *telephone systems* and *audio conference.*

speech recognition The process of analyzing the spoken word and comparing it to data held within a computer system. See also *voice data entry.*

speech synthesis The generation of speech by electronic means. See also *synthesizer* and *voice output.*

speech synthesizer A *solid state* electronic output device for generating sound similar to human speech upon the receipt of digital signals. See also *voice output.*

speed of a computer The speed of a computer quoted in terms of number of calculations, number of data transfers per second or *mips* is often used to indicate the relative processing power of a given computer system. The *CPU's* speed is dependent upon numerous factors such as *word length,* instruction set, technology of implementation and memory access times.

spelling error detection A system dictionary that can check the spelling of all words contained within a document and indicate errors.

split screen The provision of facilities that allow more than one *window* on a *screen.*

spool A reel on which magnetic tape, *paper tape* or *printer ribbon* is wound. Also a term used to mean the transfer of data intended for a peripheral device into an intermediate store. The transfer may then take place at a more convenient time, i.e. when the device is free or when sections of data have been collected together for a bulk transfer to the peripheral. See also *spooling.*

spooling The action of transferring data to an intermediate store and a method of handling virtual input and output in a *multiprogramming system.* A common problem is the slow speed of printers in relation to computer processing speeds and the need to store printer output until the device can handle it without making the process stop until printing is complete.

spreadsheet (or spreadsheet calculator) This term is usually applied to computer programs that allow figures to be entered on a grid format similar to the page of a conventional ledger book. For each position in the grid, a number or formula can be specified so that altering individual numbers can produce an alternative set of results that use the same basic principles of calculation. This makes the software very useful for modeling and planning using a 'what if' approach.

spreadsheet software Software that provides an electronic spreadsheet calculating tool that allows numeric data to be displayed in a variety of formats. This software is commonly used for preparing budgets, comparing proposals, evaluating alternatives, and making forecasts.

sprocket holes Holes provided on blank paper supplies such as paper tape and printer paper to allow a *tractor feed* device with a toothed wheel to pick up the paper and move it forward. The sprocket holes are off-center and much smaller than the punched holes on paper tape, whereas printer paper has holes punched along the edge of *continuous stationery.*

SQA See *software quality assurance.*

SRR System resource request. A routine that the application program must call to request services of the *nucleus.*

SSI See *small scale integration.*

stack A temporary area of memory used to hold sets of data. As each new item is added, the previous ones are all shifted down one place. Only the last one in may be removed at any time. Also called pushdown stack, push-down list or *LIFO* list.

stack pointer A CPU *register* that contains the *address* of the next available *stack* entry.

staged changeover See *pilot operation.*

stand-alone system A computer system or *subsystem* that is capable of operation without being connected to any other computer system or subsystem. For example, a stand-alone word processor is self contained and is provided with all the necessary components and peripherals for word processing.

stand-by facilities Reserve equipment, power generators or a duplicate set of processors that can be used in case of breakdowns. Some companies with similar equipment provide stand-by facilities for others, but if continuous processing is necessary then a company will have a duplicate set of equipment. See also *redundancy.*

standard form A *document* into which variable information (the data that varies from one situation to another) can be inserted, enabling the document to be used repeatedly in similar situations.

standard interface A point of interconnection between two systems or parts of a system. An *interface* may be classed as standard on the basis of manufacturer, industry or international usage.

standard paragraph A piece of text that can be a part of many different documents, *e.g.* a clause within a contract. It is stored on disk and brought into the text as required.

standard text See *standard paragraph.*

star network A simple network with all the links connecting directly to a single central station. Compare *ring data network* and *bus network.* Disadvantages of a star network include: central switch failure disrupts the entire network, there are no alternative routes if the link between the node and central station fails, there can be a high cost involved in directly linking every node to the center and total communication capacity is often limited by the speed of the central main switch. The main advantage is that simple terminals may be used as nodes to a star network.

state of the art In an evolving technology, the current level of development.

statement See *program statement.*

static An item incapable of changing with time.

static RAM A *RAM* in which data does not have to be refreshed. Compare *dynamic RAM.*

station See *workstation.*

stationery computer See *continuous form paper, single-feed sheet, preprinted forms* and *fanfold paper.*

statistical multiplexor See *network processor.*

status line A line at the top or bottom of the screen that gives specific information about the work or activity being undertaken by a process or application package. For example, in word processing applications it can include items like length of page, position of *margins,* allocation of *markers,* number of free characters, etc.

STD See *subscriber trunk dialing.*

stepping motor A special form of motor that produces step movements in response to digital signals, *e.g.*

providing precise movements under *microprocessor* control for applications such as *robotics.*

stop code A special character used in word processing to denote the position where information will be automatically entered at a later stage, also called start code or switch code.

storage See *memory.*

storage device A device for storage, *e.g.* magnetic tape, magnetic disk and memory.

storage disk A magnetic disk used for data or program storage.

storage location See *store location.*

storage media *Media* suitable for data storage, *e.g.* tape, disks, *nonvolatile store.*

storage tube A vacuum tube that can receive and retain information. The data can be erased and new data entered as required. The data may be text or graphics and is visible on the face of the tube.

store See *memory.*

store and forward systems A system that passes information from *node* to node in a *communication network,* pausing in each node until sufficient resources are available for the next stage of the journey.

store location The basic unit within a computer store, capable of holding a single item of data. Also called a cell.

straight insertion sort A sorting *algorithm* that looks at each *sortkey* in turn, and on the basis of this places the record corresponding to the sort key correctly with respect to the previous sortkeys.

straight selection sort A sorting *algorithm* based upon finding successively the record with the largest *sortkey* and putting it in the correct position, then the record with the next largest sortkey, etc.

stream A flow of data characterized by relatively long duration and constant rate.

strikeover Typing or keying one *character* over another.

string A set of one or more characters that the computer will hold, identify and process together.

string concatenation The linking together of sets of strings. For example, if string A holds the letters 'abcde' and string B holds the letters 'fghij,' then concatenating the strings A and B will produce a string holding 'abcdefghij.'

string function Any programming function that provides special string handling facilities, e.g. obtaining the length of a string, retrieving the ten leftmost characters of a string.

strip window A display that shows a single line of text. See also *single line display.*

structured design The strategy of dividing a design task into a number of smaller modules for development.

structured programming A method of programming that emphasizes breaking large and complex tasks into successively smaller sections. Sometimes referred to as top down programming. See also *program structure.*

structured walkthrough A formal meeting review of analysis, design or programming in order to identify errors, omissions and ambiguities in any of the documentation produced during the system development process. Walkthroughs are correspondingly focused on analysis, design, programming or testing at different stages of a project.

stylus printer Another name for a *dot matrix printer.*

subprogram A sequence of statements organized so that their combined processing can be activated by a single request (invocation) from any place in a program.

subrange A contiguous sequence of values extracted from an available repertoire of discrete values. (For example, 1.24 defines a subrange of 24 values from the repertoire of expressible positive and negative integers.)

subroutine See *subprogram.*

subroutine library A collection of frequently referenced subroutines that can be loaded with an application program.

subscriber trunk dialing (STD) The facility for a telephone subscriber to dial long distance (trunk) calls directly.

subscript A character that is printed below the baseline, *e.g.* 2 in H_20. Compare *superscript.* Also a means of referring to particular elements in an array, *e.g.* S(I) is the Ith element of the array S.

subsystem A part of a system.

super high frequency (SHF) A band of radio frequencies between 3GHz and 30GHz, usually used for microwave relays.

supercomputer Usually a class of very powerful computers that are capable of performing over 10 megaflops (million floating point instructions per second), *e.g. CRAY* and *CYBER.*

superscript A character that is printed above the baseline, *e.g.* the 3 in x^3. Compare *subscript.*

supervisor program See *executive program.*

swapping device A device, usually *backing store,* to which data is transferred when it is not in use and from which it is read when required. Swapping generally takes place in *time sharing* systems.

switch An electronic or electromechanical device that is used to connect or disconnect an electric current to an electrical circuit. Also a type of progamming branch statement with a choice of many places to which control may be passed.

switched star network An alternative to the *tree and branch network* for providing *cable television.* It is characterized by each subscriber being connected via their individual cables to a bank of central selector *switches* that they, as well as the system controller, may remotely control.

switching Various communication techniques that provide point to point transmission between dynamically changing data source and reception locations. See also *packet switching* and *message switching.*

switching circuit Another name for a *logic circuit.* Before the development of low cost electronic switching devices, a logic circuit would be implemented via relays and other electromechanical devices. An *AND function* would use two switches in series and an *OR function* two switches in parallel.

symbol table A list kept by a language *translator* of *identifiers* in a program and their properties.

symbolic address A label assigned in place of an absolute numeric address, for purposes of relocation.

synchronization A relationship between processes such that one process cannot proceed without a second process reaching a specific point. For example, when one process is writing information to a *buffer* to be read by a second process, the two processes must be synchronzied so that the reading process does not attempt to read beyond the point at which the writing process has written data into the buffer. Synchronization can be achieved by using a *semaphore.*

synchronous data link control (SDLC) A data link control protocol developed and used by IBM.

synchronous data transmission A form of data transmission whereby each byte is sent in a strict sequence, with strict timing between bytes. Especially useful at high data rates, since it is resistant to errors.

synchronous mode An operation mode that requires a form of control timing in which sequential events take place at fixed times. See also *asynchronous mode.*

synchronous transmission A system of data communications in which the timing of all devices is controlled by a single source. Synchronizing characters are sent at the start of the message to set the timing mechanism of the receiver, which is then able to count off the bits into predetermined groups.

syntax The set of rules defining the legal sequences for combining elements of a language. In the case of programming languages, the syntax defines the permitted combinations of characters to define a *statement* but does not define the meaning or use of the final construction.

syntax error This error results from the incorrect use of the rules governing the structure of the language being used. See also *syntax.*

synthesizer An output device that generates sound similar to human speech (speech synthesizer) or musical notes (music synthesizer) on receipt of digital signals.

system The term system may be applied to any combination of hardware, software, *documentation* and manual procedures that are combined to perform a specific function. For example, the contents of the computer room may be called the system, a set of programs that perform a specific application may be called a 'payroll' system and a piece of hardware that processes special text handling software may be called a *word processing* system.

system bus The group of parallel *data, address,* and control lines that connect the *CPU* to the rest of the computer system.

system crash A system failure that requires at least *operator* intervention and often some maintenance before service is restored.

system design The activity of proceeding from an identified set of system requirements to a design that meets the requirements.

system diagnostics See *diagnostic message.*

system disk A disk reserved for holding *system software.*

system environment The hardware and software organization of a microcomputer system.

system flowchart A *flowchart* used to describe a complete data processing system.

system generation (SYSGEN) A procedure that allows the user to customize the characteristics of an operating system to match the hardware available and the potential software application programs that will be run under the operating system.

system hacker See *hacker.*

system life cycle The phases of development through which a computer based application will pass from initial conception, requirements definition, outline design, detailed design, programming, testing, implementation to maintenance and modification. Some projects will also require manual procedures design and staff training.

system residence device An auxiliary storage unit on which operating system programs are stored so that they can be loaded into main storage.

system security An operating system is responsible for controlling access to system resources. Therefore the system must include protection for data and access to the part of the system that administers the protection must be specially controlled.

system software The totality of software required to produce a system acceptable to end-users.

system specification The definition of a system design in terms of required hardware and software.

system support Generally the team of people responsible for writing and maintaining the software associated with the *operating system.*

system utilities Programs that assist the user in performing certain housekeeping functions on the system.

systems analysis The study of an office process, such as accounts receivable, defining it in terms of inputs, procedures and outputs.

systems analyst A person who carries out *systems analysis* and may be responsible for producing a design, which will then be passed on for programming.

systems approach An analysis that takes into consideration the needs of the whole, not just the individual parts.

systems design The preparation of a design for a computer system that might include software specifications, equipment specifications, system configuration, staffing, training, workflow, procedures, etc.

systems furniture Modular, interchangeable office furniture components designed to accommodate computer equipment and users.

systems house A company that sells a total system, often including hardware from other suppliers.

T

T See *tera-*.

TAB See *tabulate.*

tab rack See *ruler line.*

table A data structure in the form of a rectangular arrangement of items in rows and columns, *e.g.* a two dimensional *array* or a collection of records where the rows are the individual records and the columns of data correspond to fields within a record.

table lookup (TLU) A fast method of transforming one set of data values into another. The data is stored in the form of a table. In order to perform the transformation, the original form of a value is used as an index to search the table for its corresponding new value.

tablet See *graphics tablet.*

tabulate (TAB) A means of laying out data at prescribed positions across and down a page of a display screen or printer output.

tape Either *magnetic tape* or *paper tape.*

tape deck See *magnetic tape unit.*

tape drive See *magnetic tape unit.*

tape format The format of information recorded on magnetic tape. This consists of the encoded data preceded and followed by information blocks required by the tape system.

tape header A header block of information written at the beginning of a magnetic tape.

tape library An area in which reels of magnetic tape are stored. See also *automated tape library.*

tape mechanism See *magnetic tape unit.*

tape reader See *paper tape equipment.*

tape transport See *magnetic tape unit.*

task Another name for a process.

TCM See *thermal control module.*

TCT Task control table. The table that contains entries for each task executing in a *multiprogramming system.*

technology The application of science to provide objects necessary for human sustenance and comfort.

technology agreement An agreement conceived by trade unions as a framework for negotiating conditions under which technological change takes place.

technology generations See *first, second, third, fourth* and *fifth generation computers.*

technology transfer The collaboration, awareness and special interests required to encourage industry and commerce to make good use of new technology products.

telecommunication network See *network* and *telecommunications.*

telecommunications The technology concerned with communicating at a distance. The original information energy (human voice, music, telegraphy) is converted into an electrical form which is then transmitted by line using wires and cables or by radio.

teleconference See *audio conference.*

teleconferencing Holding a meeting via telephones.

telefax The exact transmission of text and diagrams via telephone, radio or satellite links (facsimile transmission).

telematics The convergence of the disciplines in telecommunications, computer engineering, data processing and office machinery industries, *i.e.* data engineering.

telenet A public *packet network,* owned by the General Telephone and Electronics Corporation. It has been operational since 1975 and is available in the U.S.A. and some other countries. It was developed from *ARPANET* technology.

telephone answering machines Machines that 'answer' the telephone when the subscriber is busy or out. The machine makes an announcement which can be changed and may have facilities to record an incoming message, *i.e.* telephone answering/recording machines. See also *answering/recording machine.*

telephone conference See *audio conference.*

telephone systems See *private automatic branch exchange, private automatic exchange* and *private manual branch exchange.*

telephone tag Situation in which telephone calls are made and calls are returned, but the parties repeatedly miss each other.

teleprinter A device similar to a typewriter but provided with a signal interface for sending and receiving messages. Recently VDUs have tended to replace teleprinters.

teleprocessing Processing that is carried out from a *remote terminal.*

telesoftware Software transmitted by *teletext.*

telestaffing A work arrangement in which an employee inputs material into computer equipment at home and then electronically transmits it to the office.

teletex An improved *telex* service that offers higher speeds and improved quality of transmission together with better editing and processing facilities.

teletext A system of one-way broadcast transmission of information, primarily in text form with simple graphics. It uses spare television channel capacity and is broadcast *videotex.* See also *Oracle.*

teletype A trade name for a particular make of teletypewriter. The term is commonly, but wrongly, applied to any teletypewriter.

teletype network (TELNET) The *protocol* developed for the *ARPANET,* to allow users in one host computer to connect to the time sharing resources of another host.

teletypewriter An input/output device consisting of keyboard and a typewriter-like printer, often combined with a paper tape reader and punch. It can be used as a terminal or for the preparation of punched tape for subsequent input.

television (TV) A system employing photoelectrical and broadcasting processes by which an actual or recorded scene may be reproduced at a distance on a screen.

telex A service that allows users to communicate with each other using the telephone system and a *teleprinter.*

telex plus See *teletex.*

TELNET See *teletype network.*

template A cardboard or plastic plate which fits over the keyboard and contains a summary of commands for a particular software.

ten's complement The decimal number that when added to the original decimal number will give a power of 10, *e.g.* the ten's complement of 78 is 22 as 78 + 22 = 100.

tera- (T) A prefix to a unit indicating a multiple of one million million, *e.g.* 1×10^{12} bytes is a terabyte.

terminal A data input and/or output device that is connected to a controlling processor to which it is usually subservient and *remote.* See also *dumb terminal* and *intelligent terminal.*

terminal emulation A program which, when run on a microcomputer system with a video display, emulates a dumb terminal, allowing the user to access another computer. It allows access to other computers without having to reconnect cables or rearrange the system.

terminal interface processor (TIP) See *interface message processor.*

terminal operating system (TOPS) One of the *multiprogramming systems* available on Digital Equipment Corporation's larger machines, the DEC-10 and DEC-20 systems.

terminator A specified value, not normally expected in a set of data, that is used to terminate a list of data items.

terrestrial microwave transmission system A system of relay stations located about 50 km apart and in line of sight, which transmit microwave communication signals through the earth's atmosphere from one station to the next.

test data Prepared data with known results used for testing equipment and/or software.

testing Any activity that checks whether a system or component behaves in the desired manner. This is achieved by one or more test runs in which the system is supplied with input data *(test data),* and the system's responses are recorded for analysis.

testing programs The process of *testing* a program.

text Information in the form of words, sentences and paragraphs.

text editor A program used specifically for entry and modification of data that is in textual *format.* Such data may be a program written in a *high level language* or a report or book written in a *natural language.* Some editors are line oriented and some are character oriented. With screen editors, the display screen forms a movable *window* into the text, within which the *cursor* may be positioned at points where insertions, deletions and other editing functions are to be performed.

text management The provision of facilities for text creation, editing, filing, retrieval, printing and the means of handling abbreviation libraries and list processing. See also *advanced text management.*

text manipulation See *text management* and *word management.*

text processing See *word processing.*

text register A special temporary storage area for *blocks* of text that are being copied.

thermal control module (TCM) A unit that accommodates up to 133 *integrated circuits* on a 28 layer ceramic substrate. It has nearly 2000 pins per module and is water cooled.

thermal printer A type of printer in which the image is produced by the localized heating of paper that has a thin thermosensitive coating containing two separate components which melt and combine to provide a visible mark.

thermal transfer printer A printer in which thermoplastic ink is transferred to paper from a donor roll or thin backing material by localized heating.

THF See *tremendously high frequency.*

thimble A printing element similar to a *daisy wheel* but bent into a cup shape.

thimble printer An *impact printer* in which the metal printing element is cup-shaped or thimble-shaped.

thin film memory A memory device whose individual elements are formed by evaporating a thin film of magnetic material onto a glass substrate. Large capacity memories can be formed in a single operation using this process.

thin window display A single line *VDU* which displays a line of between 15 and 40 characters.

third generation computers The generic term used to describe those machines in which the integrated circuit replaced the transistor as the basic component. The most significant result was the ability to produce families of machines (ICL 1900 series, IBM 360 series, etc.) where a wide range of speed or working capacity was available in similar, compatible units. The improved computer power/size ratio was enormous. See also *first, second, fourth* and *fifth generation computers.*

tightly coupled Having to do with a *multiprocessing system* in which the processors can share main memory or disk memory and can communicate at a fairly high rate.

time sharing A technique for sharing the time of a computer between a number of users or different processing tasks. The time intervals are so small and the computer switches so rapidly that each job appears to have the computer to itself.

time sharing computer A computer that can provide *time sharing* facilities.

time slice The time limit allocated to an individual task before processing transfers to another task. See also *time sharing.*

TIOB A task I/O block that keeps track of device allocations for each task.

TIP Terminal interface processor.

tipped-on letterhead Letterhead that is spot glued to a carrier sheet in four corners. The carrier sheet feeds through a printer as continuous paper, after which the letterhead is removed.

TLU See *table lookup.*

toggle switch command The same command or key is used to turn a function on or off.

top down A method of system design or programming whereby the designer or programmer divides the problem into many small units each of which follows on from the one before. Programs are written and tested for each unit and only when a unit performs successfully is it added to the previous units. See also *structured programming.*

topology A term used to define the structural shape of a network.

top space Defines the number of lines to be left blank at the top of a page of word processed text.

TOPS See *terminal operating system.*

trace A means of checking the logic of a program by inserting statements that cause the values of variables or other information to be printed out as the program is executed. Some computers have trace software that will automatically follow each step of a program, line by line, printing the line number when the line instruction is executed.

tracing routine A routine that provides documentation of specified events and the sequence in which those events occur during execution of a *program.*

track The portion of a *magnetic storage medium* that is accessible to the *read/write heads.* The tracks on a tape are parallel to the edge of the tape. On a disk the tracks are concentric circles. On a drum the tracks are equal sized bands around the circumference.

tractor feed A mechanism for advancing paper by use of perforations (sprocket holes) and a toothed wheel (a sprocket). Compare *friction feed.*

train printer A type of *impact printer* in which the type *font* is etched or engraved upon metal slugs that are pushed around a guide track. It was finally superseded by the *band printer* and some of the newer *nonimpact printers.*

transaction A single coherent action on a file or data base.

transaction file A file containing relatively transient data, *e.g.* details of file updates which will be processed with the current master file to produce the new master file. It may also be called an update file or change file.

transaction processing The use of an on-line computer system to interrogate or update files as requested, rather than batching such requests together for subsequent processing.

transborder data flow The flow of data across national and international boundaries via international communication systems. The use of data transfer systems in this way means data can be transported around the world and yet is never produced on paper. This can lead to a breach of copyright or *data protection legislation* in the different countries.

transceiver An acronym for transmitter and receiver. A device that can both transmit and receive signals on a communication medium, *e.g. modem, terminal, codec.*

transcription The conversion of dictated material into keyed or printed form.

transcription error An error that occurs when data is being transferred from one medium to another, *e.g.* misreading handwriting as data is read and keyed into a computer. Certain conventions have been introduced to minimize errors such as between letter O and zero (a bar is drawn through the zero).

transducer Any device that converts energy from an electrical form or to an electrical form, *e.g.* a loudspeaker converts electrical energy into sound energy, a photoconductor converts light into electrical energy.

transformer An electrical device, without moving parts, which by electromagnetic induction transforms energy from one or more circuits to other circuits at the same frequency. This is usually accompanied by changes in the values of voltage and current.

transient error An error that is recoverable by the equipment's error recovery procedures. It is an error caused by a temporary malfunction, *e.g.* reading from a magnetic tape when the device is faulty but the data is still correct and may be read by a new or repaired device. Compare *hard error, permanent error.*

transient program A program that is used only briefly or only once in a great while, or one that is not resident in the operating system.

transistor A semiconductor device that acts like a switch or amplifier in an electronic circuit. In general, they have three terminals that are attached to electrode regions within the device. Current flowing between two of these electrodes is made to vary in response to voltage or current variations imposed on the third electrode. The device is capable of current or voltage amplification depending on the particular circuit implementation employed. It is used as a switch by driving it between its maximum and minimum of current flow. The transistor (derived from TRANsfer reSISTOR) was invented in 1948 by Shockley, Brattain and Bardeen at Bell Laboratories. See also *bipolar transistor, field effect transistor* and *junction transistor.*

transistor-resistor logic (TRL) The earlier logic circuits which used transistor-resistor circuitry from 1959. Now replaced by *TTL* technology.

transistor-transistor logic (TTL) A widely used family of logic circuits that are produced in integrated circuit form and whose principal switching components are *bipolar transistors.* TTL is the most commonly used technology for *SSI* and *MSI* devices due to its low cost, high speed and ready availability.

translator A program that converts a program written in one language to the equivalent program in another language, *e.g.* a *compiler.*

transmission channel A unidirectional information route for data transmission.

transmission media The two most widely used forms of transmission are *bounded media* and *free space media.*

transparency The integration of word and data processing software into a single program.

transportable computer See *portable computer.*

transposition error An error that occurs when the order of a sequence of numbers or characters is changed, *e.g.* 5134 becomes 5314. With codes, this type of error may be detected by means of *check digits.*

transputer The computer on a chip, developed by INMOS and created as a building block for a number of new *computer architectures.*

transverse mode noise *Noise* which appears from line-to-line of a power line.

tree and branch network A network whereby the communication is fed out from a single line such as a trunk cable and then individual feeder cables are connected at intervals to distribute the facilities within a local area, *e.g.* cable TV network. Compare *star network.*

tree selection sort A refinement of a *straight selection sort* that makes use of the information gained in the first step to save on the subsequent number of comparisons required.

tremendously high frequency (THF) A range of radio *frequencies* between 300GHz and 3000GHz, millimeter wave systems leading into infrared frequencies.

TRL See *transistor-resistor logic.*

true form Pertaining to the storage of a numeric value as it is initially represented.

truncation The process of approximating a number by ignoring all information beyond a set number of significant figures, *e.g.* 1.43 would be the result of truncating the number 1.4367 to two decimal places.

trunk A physical signal carrier that connects several parts of a computer system.

truth table The notation of Boolean algebra that is convenient for defining the output of a gate as a combination of inputs.

TTL See *transistor-transistor logic.*

TTS Teletypesetting code. An enhancement of the *Baudot code.* It is a six-level code, which allows for 64 different characters and other codes.

turnaround document A document prepared by computer, distributed to a customer, then returned.

turnaround time The time interval from receipt of an assignment to return of the completed job to the originator.

turnkey Pertaining to a complete system (hardware and software) designed for a specific user, the prime contractor accepting responsibility for system design and supply of hardware and software.

turtle A drawing device used by *LOGO* and related languages. It may be an electromechanical piece of equipment drawing on the floor (floor turtle), or may be simulated by graphics on a *VDU* screen (screen turtle).

turtle graphics Diagrams and graphs drawn by a *turtle.*

TV See *television.*

twisted pair Another name for ordinary telephone wire.

twos complement A method of holding negative numbers in *binary notation* so that they can be added and subtracted in the same way as for positive numbers. The twos complement of a number is always one greater than the corresponding *ones complement.*

TWX/Telex Western Union Telegraphic message services. TWX is the domestic service; Telex is international.

typeface A set of characters of a particular style and type. Also called typestyle or *font.*

U

UART Universal asynchronous receiver/transmitter. An integrated circuit that contains all circuitry required to send and receive serial data.

UHF See *ultra high frequency.*

UIM See *ultra intelligent machine.*

ULA See *uncommitted logic array.*

ultra high frequency (UHF) A range of radio *frequencies* between 300MHz and 3GHz. They are used for television transmissions and as microcomputer outputs which connect through the aerial socket for display on a television receiver.

ultra intelligent machine (UIM) The 'thinking machine' that is the ultimate development of machines with *artificial intelligence.*

unbounded media See *bounded media* and *free space media.*

unbundled A term used by equipment suppliers whereby prices are supplied for each component of a system. This usually refers to the separation of hardware from software charges. Compare *bundled.*

uncommitted logic array (ULA) This is the name given to a chip on which there are sets of *logic circuits* that have not yet been connected together. These are the basic building blocks supplied by a chip manufacturer which can have any final layer of circuit pattern superimposed in order to create a number of chip variations for different customers.

underflow This occurs when an arithmetic operation produces a result that is smaller than the allowable range of numbers that can be represented by the electronic circuitry.

underlining A feature of word processing software in which text is automatically underlined as it is entered.

universal asynchronous receiver/transmitter (UART) A logic circuit, usually an *integrated circuit,* that will convert an asynchronous serial data stream into a byte parallel form and vice versa.

universal product code (UPC) The standard *bar code* now adopted by European countries.

UNIX An operating system introduced by Bell Laboratories in 1971 for DEC PDP 11 minicomputers. It is now used widely on much larger machines and for single user microprocessor based systems.

unjustified text Text that has not been *justified.* Compare *ragged text.*

UPC See *universal product code.*

updating Any process that changes the state of a file or program package so as to bring it up to date. This would include additions of new data, changes to data already held and alterations to a program to remove minor errors (a patch) or to add new features.

uploading A way of transferring programs or data from a microcomputer system to a host or *time sharing* system. The data being transmitted is sent by means of a *serial data* link (usually telephone) to another computer system.

uppercase One mode of keyboard input that usually refers to a character set containing capital letters as well as other symbols. See also *lowercase.*

uptime The time or percentage of time during which a computer system is operating correctly.

USART Universal synchronous-asynchronous receiver/transmitter. An integrated circuit that contains all circuitry required to send and receive *serial data* either *synchronously* or *asynchronously.*

USASCII U.S.A. Standard Code for Information Interchange. See *American Standard Code for Information Interchange.*

user The operator or user of a terminal.

user area The part of the main memory of a computer that is available for use by the user's programs. A significant portion of the main memory may be dedicated to the operating system and the facilities it requires, *e.g.* buffers.

user-defined characters The programming facility to create new characters that can be subsequently used along with standard characters and symbols.

user-friendly An adjective frequently used to indicate that a system or software package has been designed for use by inexperienced people and includes one or more helpful features to assist the user.

user interface Devices and methods incorporated into hardware and software which allow the user to think and act intuitively, thus making computers more *user friendly.*

user port The socket on the back of a microcomputer that allows additional equipment to be connected. See also *port.*

utility See *utility programs.*

utility programs The collection of programs that forms part of every computer system and provides a variety of generally useful functions, including file copying and deleting, text preparation and *program cross-reference lists.*

V

V&V See *verification and validation.*

validation An input control technique used to detect any data which is inaccurate, incomplete or unreasonable. See also *verification and validation.*

value added network (VAN) A network based on transmission facilities leased from public network operators but which uses privately owned switching computers. This enables the user to add extra facilities, such as internal *electronic mail* service, to the public network services.

value added resellers (VAR) A dealer that specializes in vertical market areas in order to capture a greater share of the *OEM* market.

valve An electronic device created around 1900 in which electrodes are enclosed in glass (like a light bulb). Used in radios, television receivers and computers, it has largely been replaced by *transistors* and other semiconductor devices.

VAN See *value added network.*

VAR See *value added resellers.*

variable A string of characters that is used to denote some value stored within the computer and which may be changed during *program execution.*

variable length record A record where the number of bits or characters is not predetermined. Thus a field of information will vary in size according to current information storage requirements.

variable text The variable information which is to be inserted into a *standard form* and which differs from one form to the next.

variable word length computer A computer that does not have a fixed *word length* but operates on data of different word lengths.

VAX The most popular corporate-level *minicomputer.* Far more powerful than most personal computers, VAX is the mainstay of computers manufactured by Digital Equipment Corporation.

VDT Video display terminal. See *video display unit.*

VDU See *video display unit.*

vendor The manufacturer and/or manufacturer's representative who sells the word processing or data processing system.

verification The process of checking the accuracy of transcription of information from one media to another. This may be from paper to *punch cards,* from computer memory to magnetic tape, from a data entry keyboard into computer memory, etc. See also *verification and validation.*

verification and validation (V&V) A generic term for the complete range of checks that are performed on a system in order to increase confidence that the system is suitable for its intended purpose. This range might include a rigorous set of functional tests, performance testing, reliability testing, etc. See also *validation* and *verification.*

verifier See *verification.*

very high frequency (VHF) A band of radio *frequencies* between 30MHz and 300MHz, usually used for sound and television broadcasting.

very large scale integration (VLSI) Over one million components on a single *integrated circuit.*

very low frequency (VLF) A band of radio *frequencies* between 3kHz and 30kHz, usually used as a voice frequency band.

VHD See *video high density format.*

VHF See *very high frequency.*

video conference Two or multiway audio and *television* link-ups between individuals or groups of people. Such conferences can be held across the world using *satellite networks.*

video disk A device for storing data that looks like a long playing music record but can be used for storing computer programs and data and *television* pictures. Developments such as the *laser disk* provide better reliability and reproduction quality.

video display A display device using a *cathode ray tube* (CRT) to show character and graphic information.

video display terminal (VDT) See *video display unit.*

video display unit (VDU) An output device that can temporarily display both *graphical* and *alphanumeric* information. In most cases the image is formed from a series of horizontal lines like a television picture. A VDU is similar to a *monitor* except that it is usually associated with a *keyboard* and often used as a *terminal* to a computer.

video high density format (VHD) This method for encoding data was introduced by a Japanese company in 1978 to provide a data capacity equivalent to 180,000 pages of 2000 characters per video disk. Data is coded in the form of changes in electrical *capacitance.* The tiny *capacitors* are formed by microscopic pits in the surface of the disk. Apart from the data pits, a second set of pits is used to guide the pick-up stylus or head. The storage technique is sensitive to contamination and disks must be kept in a protective sleeve or 'caddie' at all times.

video monitor A device which enables a user to view computer output text or graphics. See also *video display unit.*

video signal In a television set, it is the video signal that provides the picture; though in the case of a television transmission entering through the aerial socket, it has to be separated from the sound. Most *microcomputers* will display their output on a television set via the aerial socket though better picture definition is obtained with a *monitor.*

video tape Magnetic tape used for the recording and subsequent display of television or film images and sound.

video terminal A *VDU* with an associated *keyboard.*

videotex The general name for information services that store, send and display text and graphics; *viewdata* is interactive videotex and *teletext* is broadcast videotex.

viewdata The generic term for interactive (two-way) systems for transmitting text or *graphics* stored in computer data bases, via the telephone network, for display on a television screen. The definition could easily apply to a number of computer network systems and *electronic mail* facilities but viewdata should be distinguishable from these other systems as it is specially intended as a simple to use, low cost information system catering to large numbers of users.

virtual A facility or resource that does not physically exist but which is simulated so that the user can act as if it does exist.

virtual disk A RAM pack which simulates the storage characteristics of a *disk drive,* but gives much faster access to stored information.

virtual machine A collection of resources that emulates the behavior of an actual machine.

virtual memory Main memory that is simulated on disk, allowing the address space of a machine to exceed the physical main memory available. Pages of memory (usually 4k bytes) are swapped in and out of real memory as needed.

virtual storage (VS) A system in which the *workspace* for a process is held partly in high speed memory and partly on some slower and cheaper *backing store* device.

virtual store access method (VSAM) An access method suitable for files with sequential or relative organization on *direct access storage devices.*

VisiCalC An electronic *spreadsheet* program.

VLF See *very low frequency.*

VLSI See *very large scale integration.*

voice data entry Human speech entered into a computer via a microphone for conversion into digital form for processing.

voice messaging A facility of a *PABX* system that provides the telephone caller with an option to record a message if the recipient does not answer the phone or the phone is engaged.

voice output This is provided by either concatenation of previously recorded words and phrases, *e.g.* speaking clock, or voice synthesis by rules. The latter is more flexible but correspondingly more complex. The computer stores a large number of empirical rules to convert text to phonemes, phonemes to parameters of a model of the human vocal tract and finally parameters to voice output. The parameters determine features such as pitch and loudness and ensure the smooth transition from one component of speech to another.

voice print The collection of data that permits specific spoken words or phrases to identify uniquely an individual.

voice recognition See *voice data entry.*

voice response Computer controlled speech output. See also *voice output.*

voice synthesis See *synthesizer* and *voice output.*

voicegram/memo An *electronic mail* facility to store and send speech mixed with text messages.

volatile memory Types of memory that lose their stored data as soon as the power is switched off, *e.g. core store* and *RAM* chips. Magnetic disk storage and *bubble memory* do not lose their data.

voltage Electrical pressure, *i.e.* the force that causes *current* to flow through an electrical *conductor.*

voltage dip A reduced amplitude of the sinusoidal voltage. The dip may last from only a few milliseconds to several seconds, depending on the type of protection in the power supply system. The magnitude of the dip depends on the severity of its cause and on the distance of the fault from the affected operational site.

voltage transient A positive and/or negative voltage peak occurring in any position on the sinusoidal voltage. The duration of the transient may be anywhere from one complete cycle to only a few microseconds. The magnitude of transient can range from just a few volts up to several thousand volts.

VS See *virtual storage.*

VSAM See *virtual storage access method.*

W

wafer The name given to a thin slice cut from a large crystal of *germanium* or *silicon.* Wafers were first used in the mid-1950s to make *transistors* which led to the *integrated circuit* or *chip* in 1959. A typical wafer would be 0.01 inch thick, 4 inches in diameter and contain 250 chips.

wait state A machine cycle inserted into the normal operation of the microprocessor when it becomes necessary to slow down and wait for a slow memory I/O device.

walkthrough A software product review performed by a formal team. A number of such reviews may be held during the lifetime of a software project covering design requirements specification, *program specification* and implementation.

WAN See *wide area network.*

warm start The restarting of a program following a stoppage, without losing data from the previous run. See also *cold start.*

wave-guide The physical container down which a wave of light or other energy may be transmitted. An *optical fiber* is sometimes called an optical wave-guide.

wavelength The distance traveled by a waveform during the periodic time for one cycle. It is measured in meters.

what you see is what you get (WYSIWYG) A term used to indicate that the equipment will correctly represent on the screen the layout and graphics that may be printed on hard copy.

wide area network (WAN) A communication network distinguished from a *local area network* because of its longer-distance communications. The term is sometimes used for the public *packet network* of a particular country or region.

wideband networks The term 'wideband' is usually taken to refer to transmission bandwidths above the telephone circuit bandwidth of 3500 *Hertz.* The wideband digital network can carry not only computer data but other signals in computer coded form including digitized speech. It relies on new technologies to provide the facilities, *e.g. satellite network* links and *optical fiber* media for transmission.

widow line The first line of a paragraph that appears by itself at the bottom of a page of text. See also *orphan line.*

Winchester disk A specific type of compact, high speed *disk drive* and high capacity, hard disk storage medium, usually associated with having the disk permanently fixed within the drive. Some *microcomputer* manufacturers are now providing *interface* facilities for increased storage using Winchester disks.

window A rectangular area on a *display screen* inside which part of an image or file is displayed. The window can be any size up to that of the screen and more than one window can be displayed at once. The process of obtaining the part of the image through the window is called windowing.

wired household A household organized around a home information and control center. The computer occupies the central position and communicates with equipment in the house using *local area networks, e.g.* home security, air conditioning, lighting, entertainment, central heating, etc.

wired program computer A digital computer, usually a special purpose one, in which the sequence of operations is fixed and cannot be self-altered. An increase in speed of operation is gained at a decrease in flexibility. See also *hardwired.*

wired society A community of *wired households.*

word A collection of bits treated as a single unit by the *central processor* of a computer. Some computers have a *word length* of 8 bits, others use 16 or 32.

word addressable Pertaining to a computer that performs operations on fixed-length words.

word division The process of dividing a word at the end of a line to provide minimal variation of the right margin. See also *hyphenation.*

word length/size The number of bits in the computer *word.*

word processing (WP) An office automation facility for computer aided authorship, editing, storage, revision and printing of text. Some systems provide abbreviation libraries and list processing linked to *electronic mail* services. See also *advanced text management* and *word processor.*

word processor The available word processing systems fall into three main categories: (1) *stand-alone systems* supporting one operator; (2) clustered systems enabling several operators to share printing and filing resources; (3) hybrid systems attached to a central *mainframe computer* or *minicomputer* and able to perform additional functions. See also *shared logic text processor.*

words per minute (WPM) A unit of measurement for the speed of writing, typing, taking dictation or keying data.

wordwrap See *wraparound.*

work area Another name for *workspace.*

work disk (data disk, file disk) The disk on which a user stores work.

work file A file that is used to provide temporary storage space for data that is required only for the lifetime of one job, *e.g.* data that is being sorted.

working store See *scratchpad.*

workspace A block of *locations* within the main memory of a computer that are used for the temporary storage of data during processing.

workstation An operator work location that is equipped with all of the facilities required to perform a particular type of task. In data processing and *office systems* the basic electronic equipment would normally be a *visual display unit* and *keyboard.* Increasingly this will be supplemented by ancillary *storage devices, printers, bar code readers* and communication facilities ranging from automated telephone facilities to *facsimile transmission* and *teletex* services.

WORM Write once, read many. Used particularly in reference to optical disks.

WP See *word processing.*

WPM See *words per minute.*

wraparound A feature of VDU/print equipment and word processing software whereby a word that does not fit on the end of a line is automatically carried over to the next line. When word processing, an operator does not have to end any line manually except to force the start of a new line.

write head See *read/write head.*

write-permit ring A ring that is attached to the hub of a reel of magnetic tape to permit the contents of the tape to be overwritten or erased.

write-protect tab A tab that covers a small cut-out area on a *floppy disk* and thus prevents any software from overwriting or erasing the information on the disk.

writing pad This device can 'read' numbers and alphabetic characters that have been handprinted onto a form placed over the writing pad or tablet.

WYDINYA Prefix followed by a suggestion invariably employed by the first observer of a recently completed software package and relating to a minor change in screen display which would necessitate restructuring of the entire program.

wye A three-phrase source or load connection with a single common junction and three phase lines out or in.

wye-connection A standard 3-wire *transformer* connection with similar ends of the single-phase coils connected. This common point forms the electrical neutral point and may be grounded.

wye-delta The interconnections between a wye source and a *delta* load.

wye-wye The interconnections between a wye source and a wye load.

WYSIWYG What you see is what you get. In other words, the screen displays the document as it will appear on the printout.

X,Z

X.25 The *CCITT* standard *interface protocol* for *packet switching* networks that defines the message structure required by data terminal equipment.

x-y recorder See *x-y plotter.*

xerographic laser printer See *xerographic printer.*

xerographic printer This printer uses a dry copying process to print a page at a time. The image is projected onto a light sensitive plate using a *laser* beam and the plate is covered with powder which is then transferred to the paper. Such printers are capable of high speeds (20 pages per minute), good *high resolution graphics* and offer good color but are expensive. See also *electrophotographic printer.*

XON-XOFF protocol A standard *protocol* used when information is being transferred from one computer to another. It usually requires a *full duplex* data link.

x-y plotter An instrument for drawing lines on paper, often used to draw two dimensional graphic output from a computer. On some instruments the pen moves in both x and y directions on a fixed paper surface whereas other devices enable the paper to move in the x direction while the pen moves across the paper in the y direction. Generally the x-y plotter is provided with coordinates for the start and finish points of a line. However an x-y recorder requires a series of x,y increments to move the drawing head. See also *drum plotter.*

zero supression The elimination of nonsignificant zeros. While numerical data is being processed it may be expanded to a uniform number of digits by the addition of nonsignificant zeros to the left of the *most significant digit.* For printout or display these nonsignificant zeros are suppressed.

zone This generally refers to specific regions on a punched card or can refer to print/display positions, *e.g.* in *BASIC, variables* separated by commas are printed in separate zones.

Appendix A: Abbreviations and Acronyms

AC	Alternating Current
ACE	Automatic Computing Engine
ACIA	Asynchronous Communications Interface Adapter
A/D	Analog to Digital
ADC	Analog to Digital
ADCCP	Advanced Data Communication Control Procedure
ADP	Automatic Data Processing
AFIPS	American Federation of Information Processing Societies, Inc.
AHPL	A Hardware Progamming Language
AI	Artificial Intelligence
ALGOL	ALGOrithmic Language
ALU	Arithmetic and Logic Unit
AMA	Automatic Message Accounting
AMT	Advanced Manufacturing Technology
ANSI	American National Standards Institute
APL	A Programming Language
APT	Automatically Programmed Tools (language)
ASCC	Automatic Sequence Controlled Calculator
ASCII	American Standard Code for Information Interchange
ASME	American Society of Mechanical Engineers
ASR	Automatic Send and Receive
ATL	Automated Tape Library
ATM	Automatic Teller Machines

BASIC	Beginner's All-purpose Symbolic Instruction Code
BCD	Binary Coded Decimal
BDOS	Basic Disk Operating System
BIO	Byte-oriented Input/Output
BIOS	Basic Input/Output System
BIT	Binary dig-IT
BOT	Beginning of Tape
BPS	Bits Per Second
CAD	Computer Aided/assisted Design
CAE	Computer Aided/assisted Engineering
CAFS	Contents Addressable File Store
CAI	Computer Aided/assisted Instruction
CAL	Computer Aided/assisted Learning
CALL	Computer Aided/assisted Language Learning
CAM	Computer Aided/assisted Manufacturing
CAMA	Centralized Automatic Message Accounting
CAT	Computerized Aided/assisted Testing
CAT	Computer Aided/assisted Training
CBL	Computer Based Learning
CBMS	Computer Based Message Systems
CBT	Computer Bases Training
CCP	Console Command Processor
CIM	(1) Computer Input Microfilm (2) Computer Integrated Manufacturing
CIS-COBOL	Compact Interactive Standard-COBOL
CM	Central Memory
CMI	Computer Managed Instruction
CML	Computer Managed Learning
COBOL	COmmon Business Oriented Language
CODASYL	Conference on DAta SYstems Languages
COM	Computer Output on Microfilm
COMAL	COMmon Algorithmic Language
CP/M	Control Program/Monitor
CPI	Characters Per Inch
CPS	Characters Per Second

CPU	Central Processing Unit
CR	Carriage Return
CRC	Cyclic Redundancy Check
CR/LF	Carriage Return/Line Feed
CRT	Cathode Ray Tube
CSMA/CD	Carrier Sense Multiple Access/Collision Detection
CTI	Current Task Indicator
CU	Control Unit
CWP	Communicating Word Processor
DAC	Digital to Analog Converter
DASD	Direct Access Storage Device
DBMS	Data Base Management System
DBS	Direct Broadcasting by Satellite
DC	Direct Current
DCE	Data Communications Equipment
DDCMP	Digital Data Communications Message Protocol
DD/D	Data Dictionary/Directory
DDE	Direct Data Entry
DDCMP	Digital Data Communications Message Protocol
DDL	Data Description Language
DFD	Data Flow Diagram
DIL	Dual In-Line package
DIP	Dual In-line Package
DMA	Dual Memory Access
DML	Data Manipulation Language
DOS	Disk Operating System
DP	Data Processing
DSD	Data Structure Diagram
DSS	Decision Support System
DTE	Data Terminal Equipment
DTL	Diode Transistor Logic
EAPROM	Electrically Alterable Programmable Read Only Memory
EAROM	Electrically Alterable Read Only Memory

EBCDIC	Extended Binary-Coded Decimal Interchange Code
ECL	Emitter Coupled Logic
EDP	Electronic Data Processing
EDSAC	Electronic Delay Storage Automatic Computer
EDVAC	Electrical Discrete Variable Automatic Computer
EEROM	Electrically Erasable Read Only Memory
EFTS	Electronic Funds Transfer System
EHF	Extremely High Frequency
EIA	Electronics Industries Association
ELF	Extremely Low Frequency
ELT	Electronic Typewriter
ENIAC	Electronic Numerical Integrator And Calculator
EOB	End of Block
EOD	End of Data
EOF	End of File
EOJ	End of Job
EOR	End of Record
EOT	End of Tape
EPROM	Erasable Programmable Read Only Memory
ERNIE	Electronic Random Number Indicator Equipment
EVFU	Electronic Vertical Format Unit
EXNOR	EXclusive NOR
EXOR	EXclusive OR
FAX	Facsimile transmission
FCB	File Control Block
FCC	Federal Communications Commission
FET	Field Effect Transistor
FF	(1) Flip-Flop (2) Form Feed
FIFO	First In-First Out
FM	Frequency Modulation
FMS	(1) Flexible Machining System (2) Flexible Manufacturing System

G	Giga
GIGO	Garbage In, Garbage Out
HDLC	High level Data Link Control
HF	High Frequency
HFFC	Horizontal Form Flow Chart
HMI	Human-Machine Interaction or Interface
IAL	International Algorithmic Language
IAR	Instruction Address Register
IAS	Institute for Advanced Study Computer
IBG	InterBlock Gap
IC	Integrated Circuit
IDA	Integrated Digital Access
IDP	Integrated Data Processing
IEEE	Institute of Electrical and Electronic Engineers
IFIP	International Federation for Information Processing
IH	Interrupt Handler
IIL	Integrated Injection Logic
ILF	Infra Low Frequency
INTELSAT	INternational TELecommunications SATellite consortium
I/O	Input/Output
IP	Information Provider
IPL	Initial Program Load
ISBN	International Standard Book Number
ISDN	Integrated Services Digital Network
ISO	International Standards Organization
ISR	Information Storage and Retrieval
IT	Information Technology
ITSO	International Telecommunications Satellite Organization (Intelsat)
ITU	International Telecommunications Union
IVI	Interactive Video Instruction
JCL	Job Control Language
LAN	Local Area Network
LAP	Link Access Protocol

LCD	Liquid Crystal Display
LED	Light Emitting Diode
LF	(1) Line Feed (2) Low Frequency
LIFO	Last In-First Out
LISP	LISt Processing
LPM	Lines Per Minute
LQ	Letter Quality
LSB	Least Significant Bit
LSI	Large Scale Integration
M	Mega
m	Milli
MAR	Memory Address Register
MATS	Mobile Automatic Telephone System
MB	MegaByte
MBR	Memory Buffer Register
MDR	Memory Data Register
MF	Medium Frequency
MICR	Magnetic Ink Character Recognition
Mips	Million Instructions Per Second
MIS	Management Information System
MMI	Man-Machine Interface
MODEM	MOdulator-DEModulator
MPU	Microprocessor Unit
MSB	Most Significant Bit
MSD	Most Significant Digit
MS-DOS	MicroSoft Disk Operating System
MSI	Medium Scale Integration
MSR	Marketing Support Representative
MTBF	Mean Time Between Failures
MTL	Merged Transistor Logic
MTU	Magnetic Tape Unit
MX queue	Mutually eXclusive queue
n	Nano
NBCD	Natural Binary Coded Decimal
NC	Numerical Control
NLQ	Near Letter Quality
NTSC	National Television Systems Committee

OA	Office Automation
OCR	Optical Character Recognition
OMR	Optical Mark Reading
OP-AMP	OPerational AMPlifier
OP-CODE	OPeration CODE
OR	Operational Research
OS	Operating System
OSI	Open System Interconnection
OS/2	Operating System for IBM PS/2 series
p	Pico
PABX	Private Automatic Branch eXchange
PAX	Private Automatic eXchange
PBX	Private Branch eXchange
PC	Personal Computer
PCB	Printed Circuit Board
PDL	Program Design Language
PIA	Peripheral Interface Adapter
PID	Personal Identification Device
PIN	Personal Identification Number
PIO	Parallel Input/Output
PIP	Peripheral Interchange Program
PIPO	Parallel Input, Parallel Output
PISO	Parallel Input, Serial Output
PIXEL	PIcture ELement
PL/1	Programming Language 1
PLA	Programmable Logic Array
PL/M	Programming Language for Microprocessors
PMBX	Private Manual Branch eXchange
POL	Problem Oriented Language
POS	Point of Sale
.PRL	Page-ReLocatable file
PROM	Programmable Read Only Memory
PSS	Packet Switch Stream
RAM	Random Access Memory
RF	Radio Frequency
RJE	Remote Job Entry

RMS	Root Mean Square
ROM	Read Only Memory
ROS	Read Only Storage
RPG	Report Program Generator
RTL	Resistor-Transistor Logic
S-100	Standard bus
SDLC	Synchronous Data Link Control
SDT	System Device Table
SHF	Super High Frequency
SIO	Serial Input/Output
SIPO	Serial Input, Parallel Output
SISO	Serial Input, Serial Output
SOS	Silicon On Sapphire
SQA	Software Quality Assurance
SRR	System Resource Request
SSI	Small Scale Integration
STD	Subscriber Trunk Dialing
t	Tera
TAB	Tabulate
TCM	Thermal Control Module
TCT	Task Control Table
TELNET	TELetype NETwork
THF	Tremendously High Frequency
TIOB	Task I/O Block
TIP	Terminal Interface Processor
TLU	Table Lookup
TOPS	Terminal OPerating System
TRL	Transistor-Register Logic
TTL	Transistor-Transistor Logic
TTS	TeleTypeSetting code
TV	Television
TWX/Telex	Western Union TELegraphic message services
UART	Universal Asynchronous Receiver/Transmitter. An integrated circuit that contains all circuitry required to send and receive serial data.

UHF	Ultra High Frequency
UIM	Ultra Intelligent Machine
ULA	Uncommitted Logic Array
UPC	Universal Product Code
USART	Universal Synchronous-Asynchronous Receiver/Transmitter
USASCII	USA Standard Code for Information Interchange
V&V	Verification and Validation
VAN	Value Added Network
VAR	Value Added Resellers
VDT	Visual Display Terminal
VDU	Visual Display Unit
VFU	Vertical Format Unit
VHD	Video High Density
VHF	Very High Frequency
VLF	Very Low Frequency
VLSI	Very Large Scale Integration
VS	Virtual Storage
VSAM	Virtual Storage Access Memory
WAN	Wide Area Network
WORM	Write Once, Read Many
WP	Word Processing
WPM	Words Per Minute
WYSIWYG	What You See Is What You Get

Appendix B: ASCII Character Codes

The following table lists ASCII codes for letters, digits and symbols in both decimal and hexadecimal equivalents. Access commands to the ASCII system vary, depending on the program being used. Some codes are reserved for special commands. For example, ASCII decimal codes 0 to 31 often are used for the program's control functions or communications, so those codes are not presented here.

Character	ASCII Decimal	ASCII Hexadecimal
A (a)	065 (097)	41 (61)
B (b)	066 (098)	42 (62)
C (c)	067 (099)	43 (63)
D (d)	068 (100)	44 (64)
E (e)	069 (101)	45 (65)
F (f)	070 (102)	46 (66)
G (g)	071 (103)	47 (67)
H (h)	072 (104)	48 (68)
I (i)	073 (105)	49 (69)
J (j)	074 (106)	4A (6A)
K (k)	075 (107)	4B (6B)
L (l)	076 (108)	4C (6C)
M (m)	077 (109)	4D (6D)
N (n)	078 (110)	4E (6E)
O (o)	079 (111)	4F (6F)
P (p)	080 (112)	50 (70)
Q (q)	081 (113)	51 (71)
R (r)	082 (114)	52 (72)
S (s)	083 (115)	53 (73)
T (t)	084 (116)	54 (74)
U (u)	085 (117)	55 (75)
V (v)	086 (118)	56 (76)
W (w)	087 (119)	57 (77)
X (x)	088 (120)	58 (78)
Y (y)	089 (121)	59 (79)
Z (z)	090 (122)	5A (7A)

Character	ASCII Decimal	ASCII Hexadecimal
0	048	30
1	049	31
2	050	32
3	051	33
4	052	34
5	053	35
6	054	36
7	055	37
8	056	38
9	057	39
!	033	21
@	064	40
#	035	23
$	036	24
%	037	25
&	038	26
*	042	2A
(	040	28
)	041	29
-	045	2D
__	095	5F
+	043	2B
=	061	3D
:	058	3A
;	059	3B
”	034	22
’	039	27
•	060	3C
□	062	3E
?	063	3F
,	044	2C
.	046	2E
/	047	2F

Appendix C: Decimal/Hexadecimal Conversions

Hexarithmetic Column

1		2		3		4	
Dec Base	**Hex Base**	**Dec Base**	**Hex Base**	**Dec Base**	**Hex Base**	**Dec Base**	**Hex Base**
0	0		-0		-00		-000
1	1	16	10	256	100	4,096	1000
2	2	32	20	512	200	8,192	2000
3	3	48	30	768	300	12,288	3000
4	4	64	40	1,024	400	16,384	4000
5	5	80	50	1,280	500	20,480	5000
6	6	96	60	1,536	600	24,576	6000
7	7	112	70	1,792	700	28,672	7000
8	8	128	80	2,048	800	32,768	8000
9	9	144	90	2,304	900	36,864	9000
10	A	160	A0	2,560	A00	40,960	A000
11	B	176	B0	2,816	B00	45,056	B000
12	C	192	C0	3,072	C00	49,152	C000
13	D	208	D0	3,328	D00	53,248	D000
14	E	224	E0	3,584	E00	57,344	E000
15	F	240	F0	3,840	F00	61,440	F000

Computers use bytes for information storage and retrieval. Each byte holds 16 informational bits, which are equivalent to a hexadecimal numbering system. The hexadecimal system uses numerals zero through nine, plus letters A through F.

To convert a decimal number into its hexadecimal equivalent is a process of subtractions. For example, suppose that the decimal number 22,952 is to be converted to the hexadecimal system. Begin with the largest decimal number that is less than 22,952 in the table: 20,480 is equivalent to 5 (in column four), so this hexadecimal will have four digits.

Next, subtract 20,480 from 22,952 to get the next column's arithmetic equivalent. The result is 2,472 and its closest lesser equivalent in column three is 2,304 or the digit 9. The hexadecimal equivalent is now 59___.

Subtracting 2,304 from 2,472 yields 168, which is equivalent to 160, or A in column two, with 8 left over. The hexadecimal equivalent becomes 59A_. In the first column, 8 is 8. So, 22,592 is equivalent to 59A8 in the hexadecimal system.

Conversion of a hexadecimal to a decimal, simply reverses the process by adding each number. For example, the hexadecimal number F9A is 3,840 (column three) plus 144 (column two) plus 10 (column 1). So, F9A equals 3,994.